FOR ORGANS, PIANOS & ELECTRONIC KEYBOARDS

E-Z PLAY TODAY

30

COUNTRY CONNECTION

ISBN 978-0-7935-1525-7

HAL•LEONARD®

7777 W. BLUEMOUND RD. P.O. BOX 13819 MILWAUKEE, WI 53213

E-Z Play® Today Music Notation © 1975 HAL LEONARD LLC
E-Z PLAY and EASY ELECTRONIC KEYBOARD MUSIC are registered trademarks of HAL LEONARD LLC.

Visit Hal Leonard Online at
www.halleonard.com

Registration Guide

- Match the Registration number on the song to the corresponding numbered category below. Select and activate an instrumental sound available on your instrument.

- Choose an automatic rhythm appropriate to the mood and style of the song. (Consult your Owner's Guide for proper operation of automatic rhythm features.)

- Adjust the tempo and volume controls to comfortable settings.

Registration

1	Mellow	Flutes, Clarinet, Oboe, Flugel Horn, Trombone, French Horn, Organ Flutes
2	Ensemble	Brass Section, Sax Section, Wind Ensemble, Full Organ, Theater Organ
3	Strings	Violin, Viola, Cello, Fiddle, String Ensemble, Pizzicato, Organ Strings
4	Guitars	Acoustic/Electric Guitars, Banjo, Mandolin, Dulcimer, Ukulele, Hawaiian Guitar
5	Mallets	Vibraphone, Marimba, Xylophone, Steel Drums, Bells, Celesta, Chimes
6	Liturgical	Pipe Organ, Hand Bells, Vocal Ensemble, Choir, Organ Flutes
7	Bright	Saxophones, Trumpet, Mute Trumpet, Synth Leads, Jazz/Gospel Organs
8	Piano	Piano, Electric Piano, Honky Tonk Piano, Harpsichord, Clavi
9	Novelty	Melodic Percussion, Wah Trumpet, Synth, Whistle, Kazoo, Perc. Organ
10	Bellows	Accordion, French Accordion, Mussette, Harmonica, Pump Organ, Bagpipes

CONTENTS

Abilene

Registration 4
Rhythm: Swing

Words and Music by Lester Brown,
John D. Loudermilk and Bob Gibson

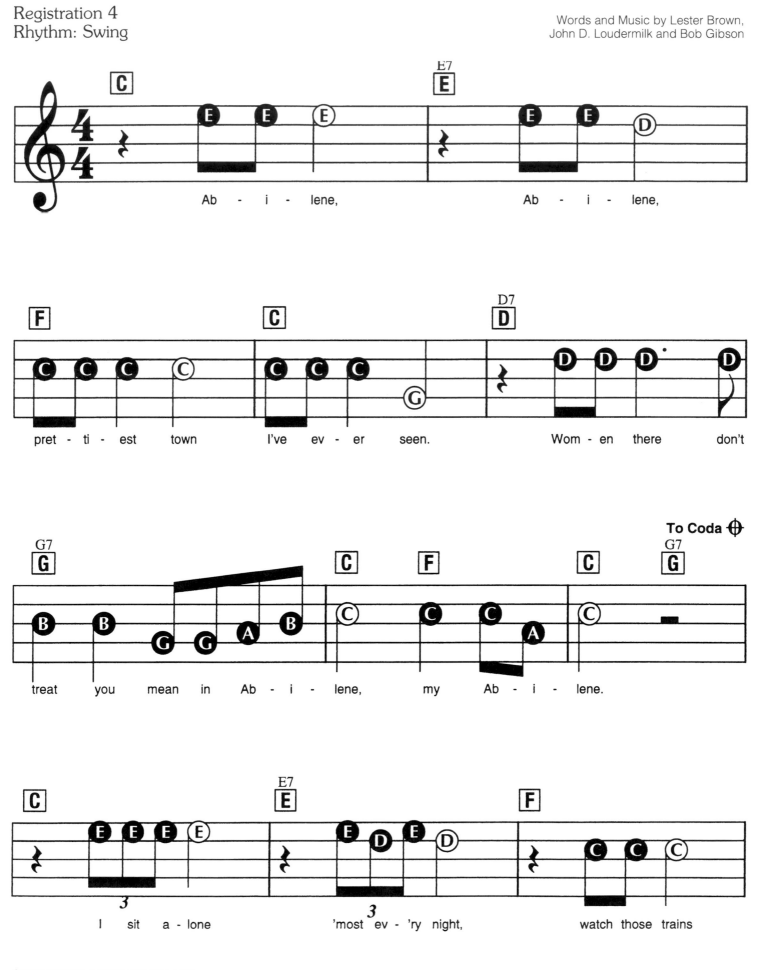

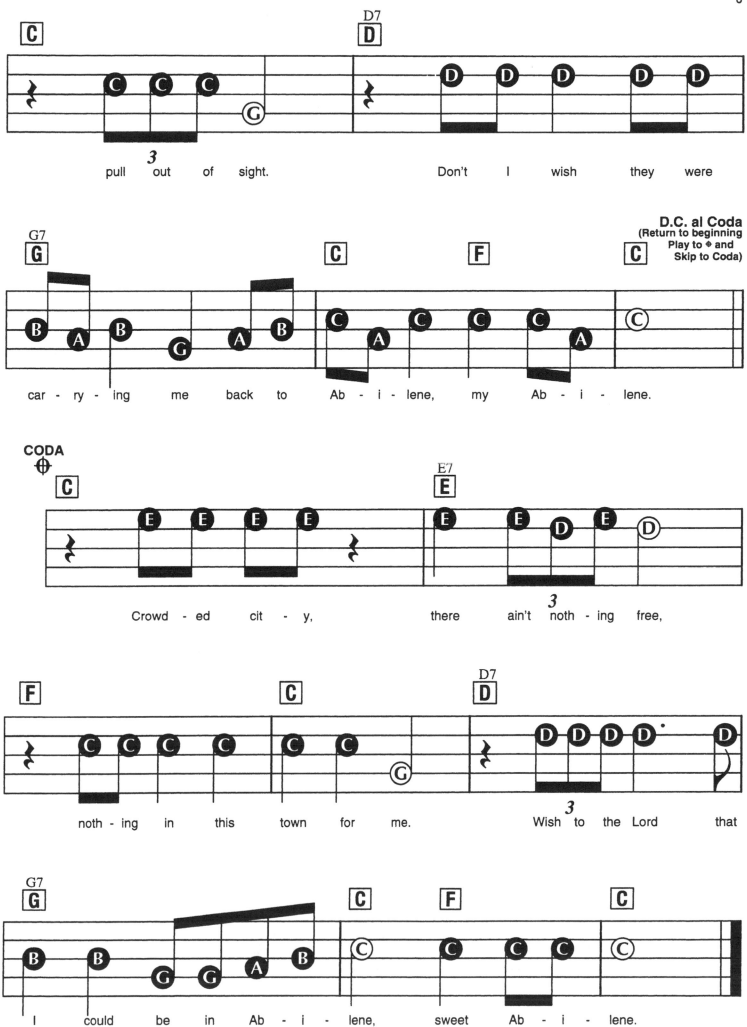

Achy Breaky Heart
(Don't Tell My Heart)

Registration 5
Rhythm: Rock or 8-Beat

Words and Music by
Don Von Tress

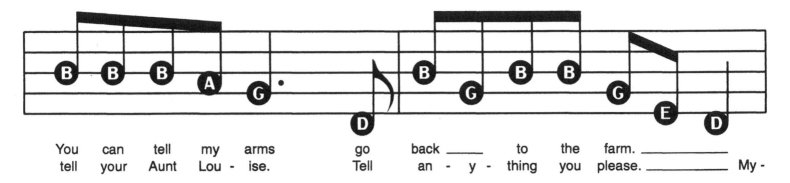

You can tell my arms go back _____ to the farm. _____
tell your Aunt Lou - ise. Tell an - y - thing you please. _____ My -

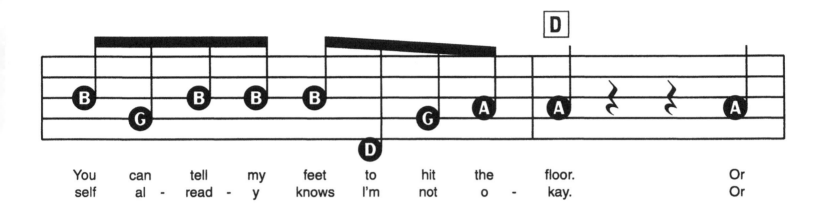

You can tell my feet to hit the floor. Or
self al - read - y knows I'm not o - kay. Or

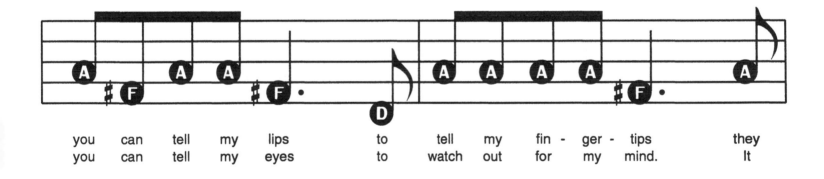

you can tell my lips to tell my fin - ger - tips they
you can tell my eyes to watch out for my mind. It

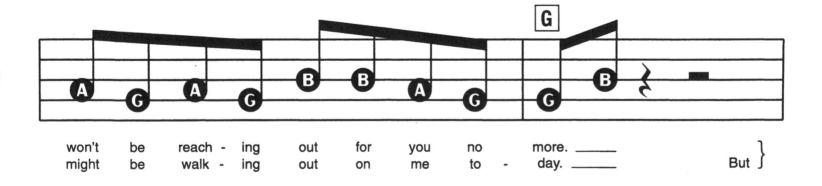

won't be reach - ing out for you no more. _____
might be walk - ing out on me to - day. _____ But

8

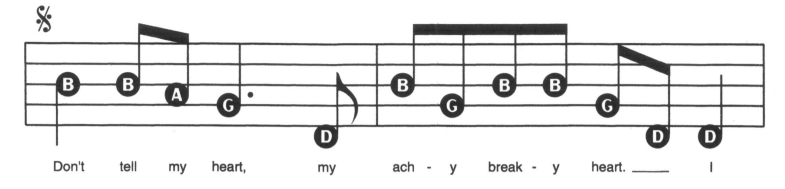

Don't tell my heart, my ach - y break - y heart. _____ I

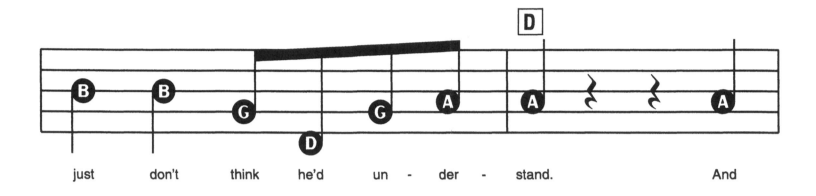

just don't think he'd un - der - stand. And

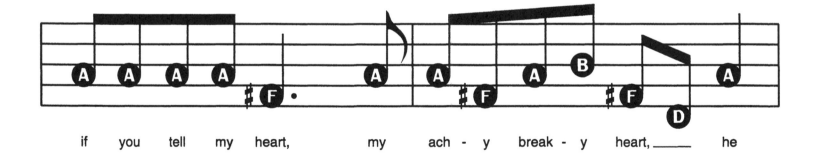

if you tell my heart, my ach - y break - y heart, _____ he

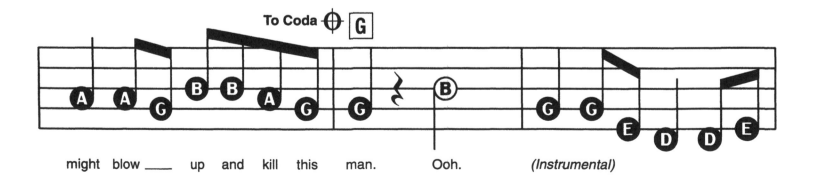

might blow _____ up and kill this man. Ooh. *(Instrumental)*

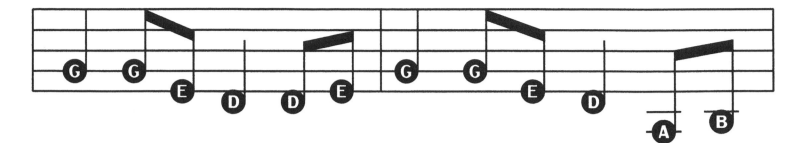

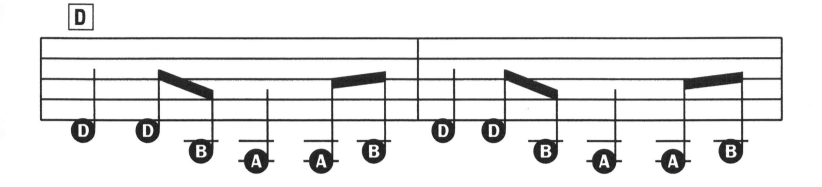

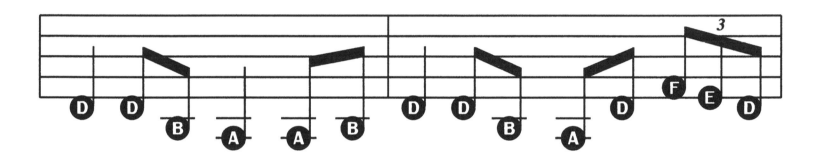

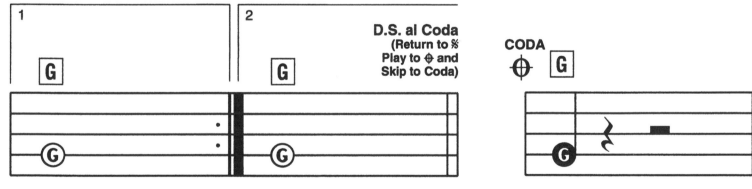

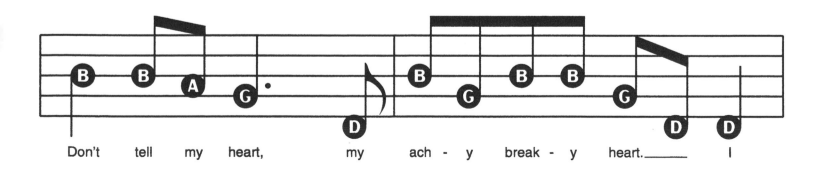

Don't tell my heart, my ach - y break - y heart._____ I

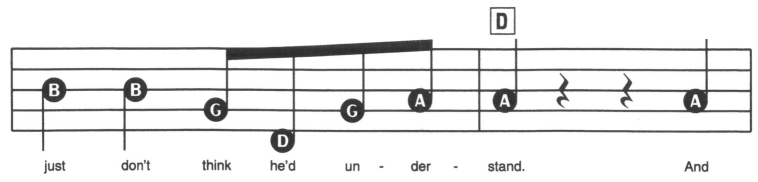

just don't think he'd un - der - stand. And

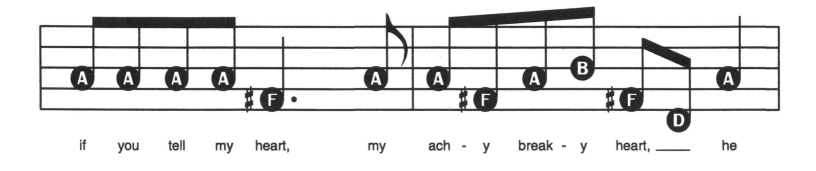

if you tell my heart, my ach - y break - y heart, _____ he

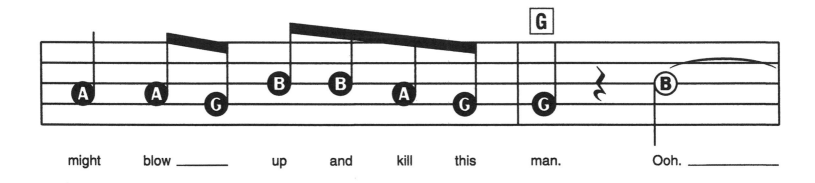

might blow _____ up and kill this man. Ooh. _____

Bless the Broken Road

Registration 1
Rhythm: Country Rock or Rock

Words and Music by Marcus Hummon,
Bobby Boyd and Jeff Hanna

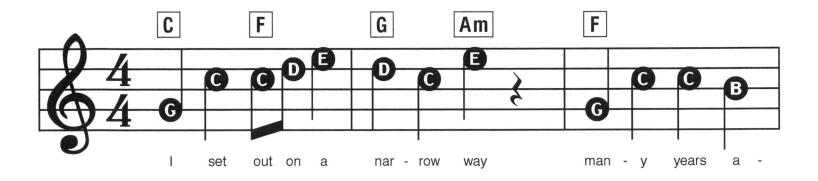

I set out on a nar - row way many years a -

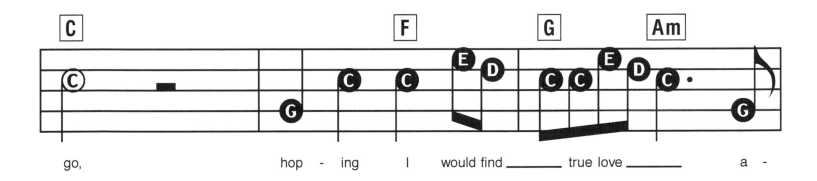

go, hop - ing I would find _____ true love _____ a -

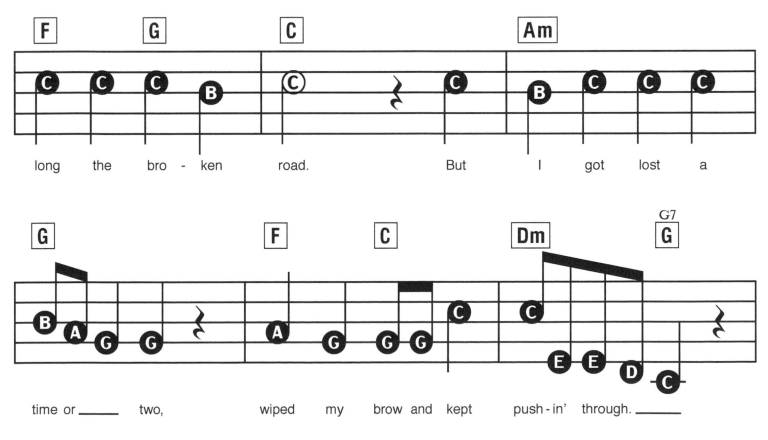

long the bro - ken road. But I got lost a

time or _____ two, wiped my brow and kept push - in' through. _____

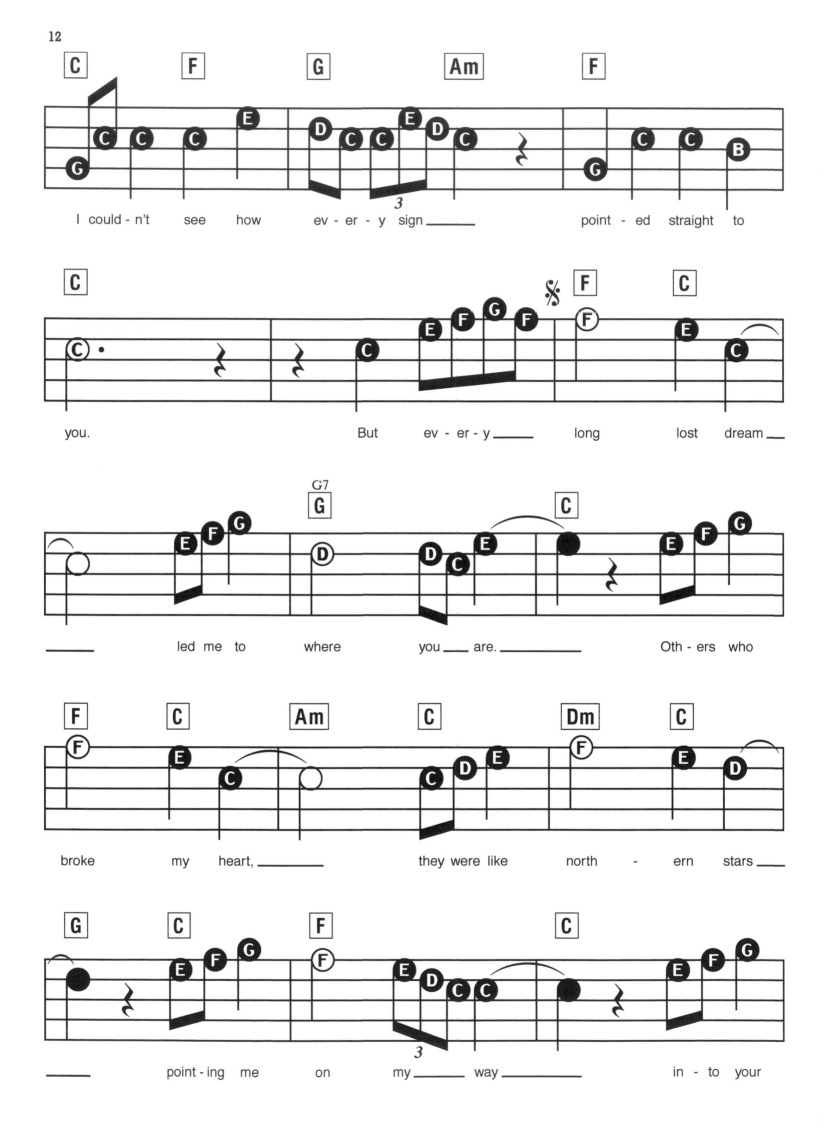

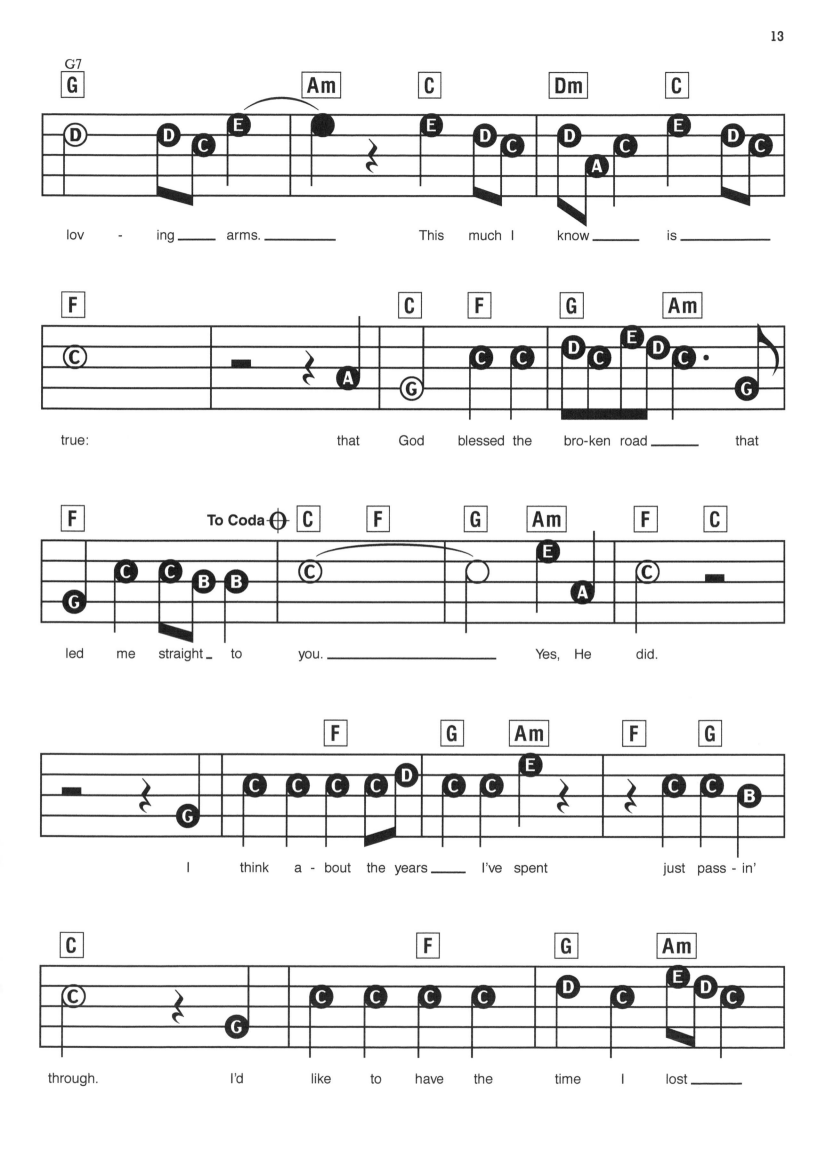

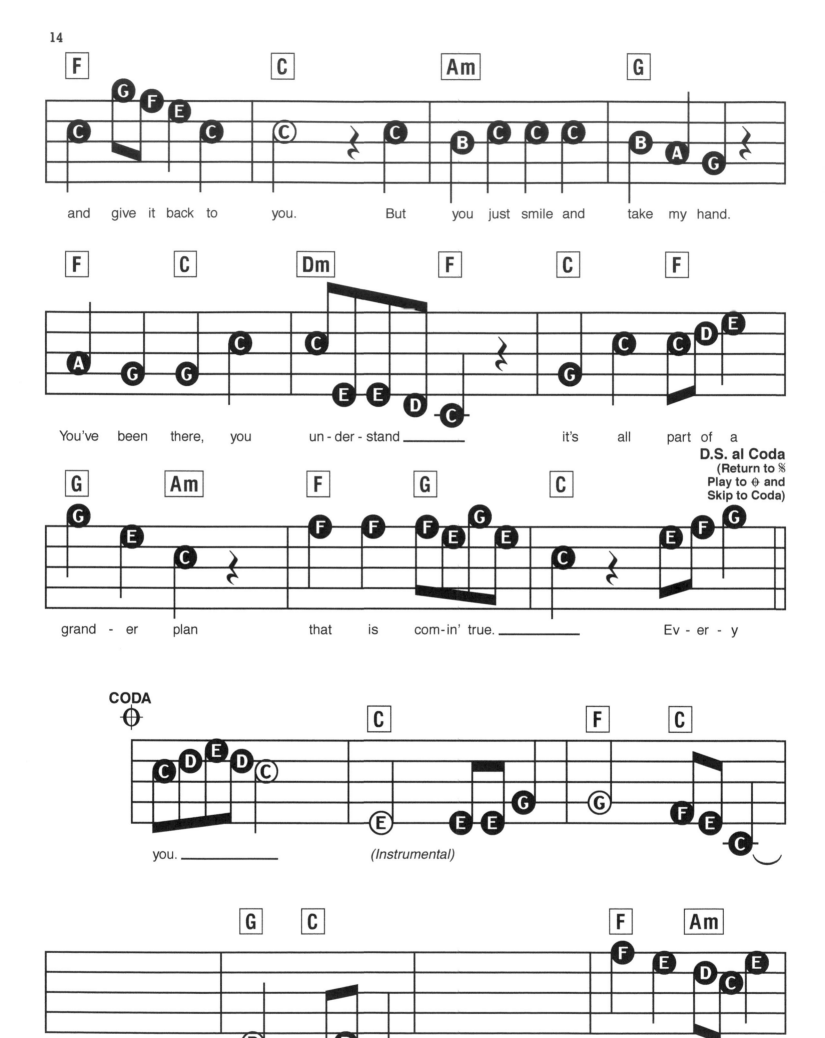

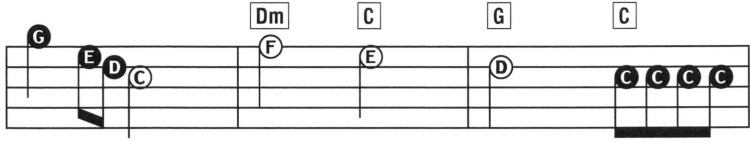

Now I'm just a -

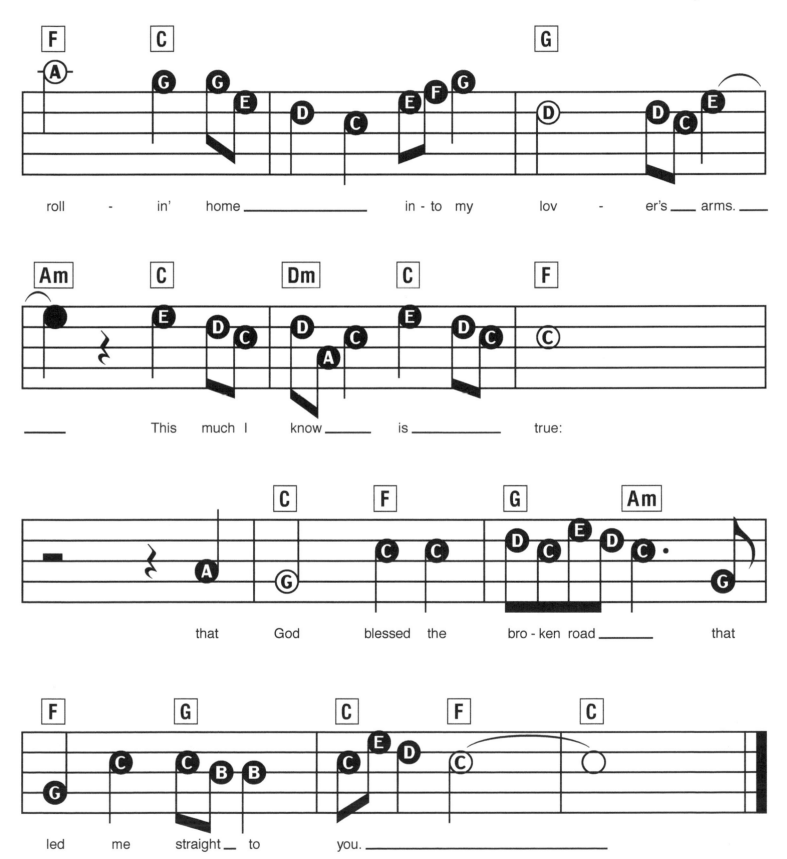

roll - in' home _____ in - to my lov - er's ___ arms. ___

_____ This much I know _____ is _____ true:

that God blessed the bro - ken road _____ that

led me straight __ to you. _____

All My Ex's Live in Texas

Registration 4
Rhythm: Country or Shuffle

Words and Music by Lyndia J. Shafer
and Sanger D. Shafer

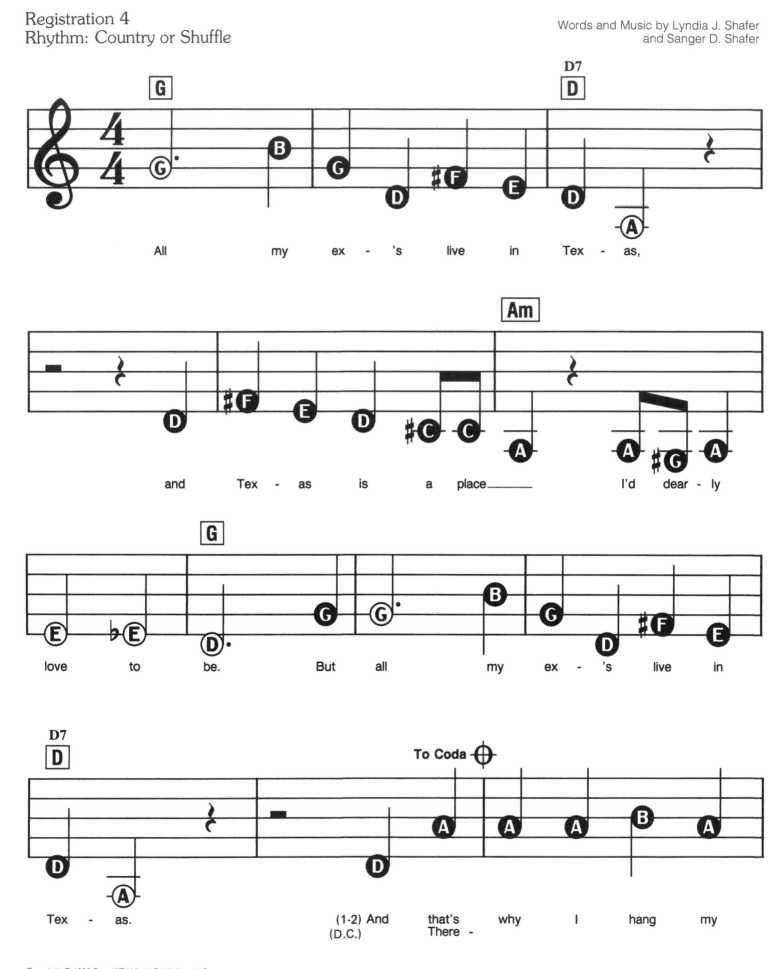

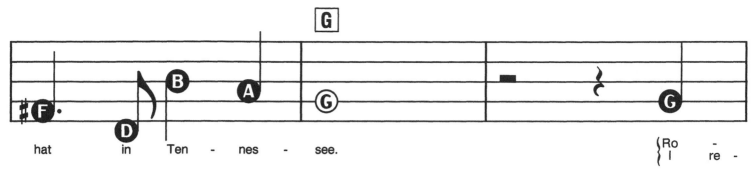

hat in Ten - nes - see. {Ro -
{I re -

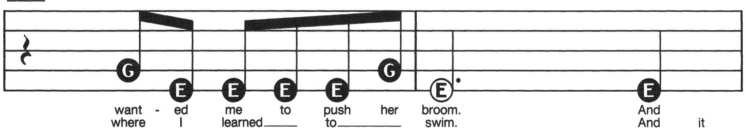

san - na's down in Tex - ar - ka - na;
mem - ber down that in old Fri - o - Riv - er

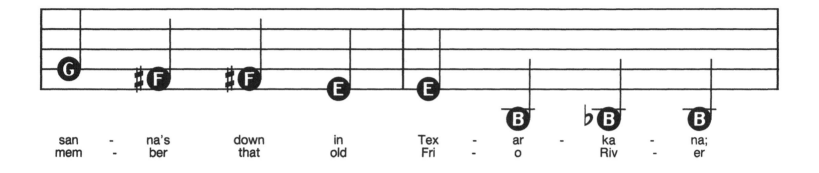

want - ed me to push her broom. And
where I learned to swim. And it

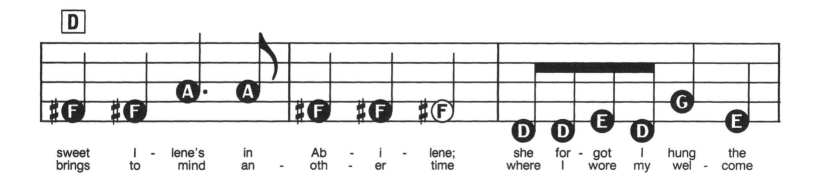

sweet I - lene's in Ab - i - lene; she for - got I hung the
brings to mind an - oth - er time where I wore my wel - come

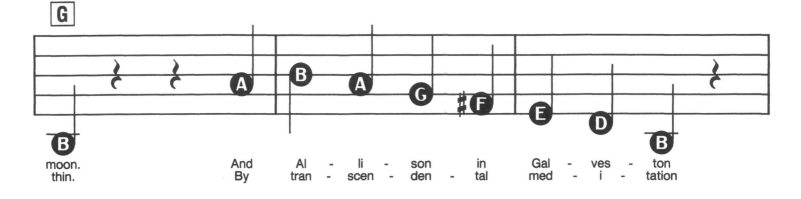

moon.
thin.
And Al - li - son in Gal - ves - ton
By tran - scen - den - tal med - i - tation

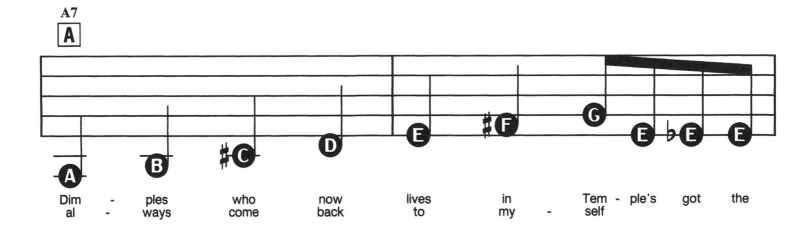

some - how lost her san - i - ty. And
I go there___ each___ night. But I

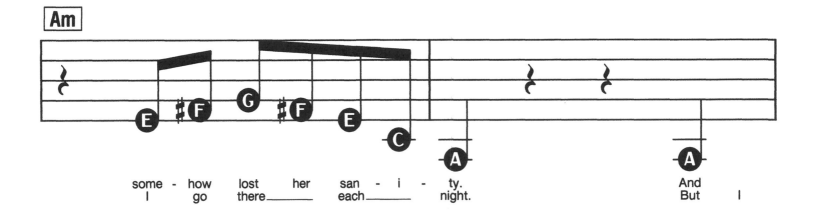

Dim - ples who now lives in Tem - ple's got the
al - ways come back to my - self

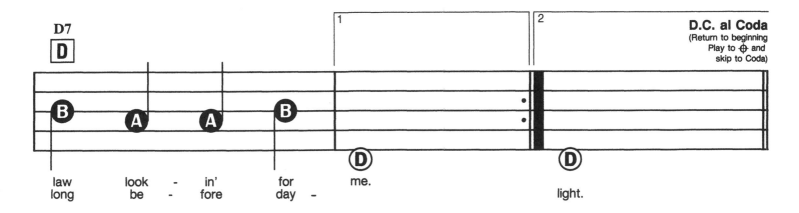

D.C. al Coda
(Return to beginning
Play to ⊕ and
skip to Coda)

law look - in' for me.
long be - fore day - light.

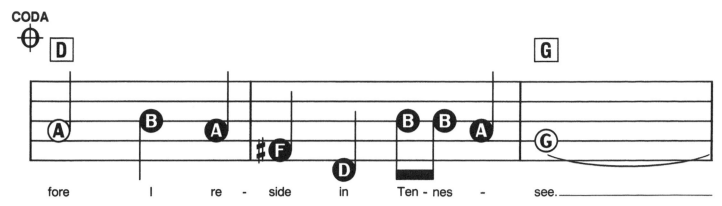

fore I re - side in Ten - nes - see. _____

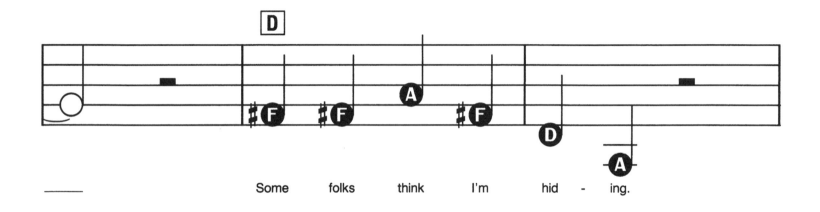

_____ Some folks think I'm hid - ing.

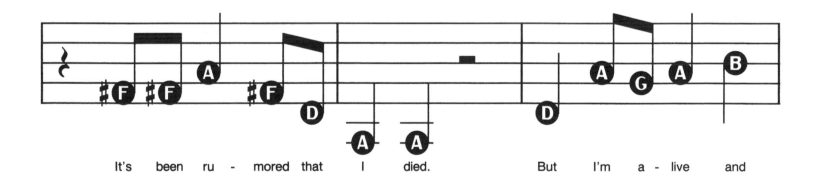

It's been ru - mored that I died. But I'm a - live and

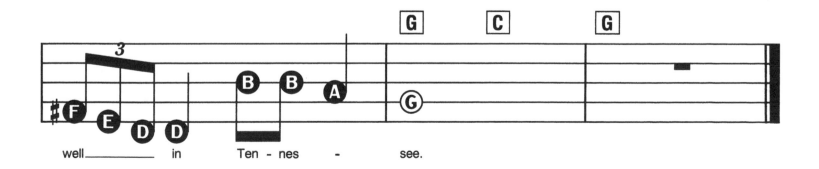

well _____ in Ten - nes - see.

Born to Lose

Registration 1
Rhythm: Country Swing or Fox Trot

Words and Music by
Ted Daffan

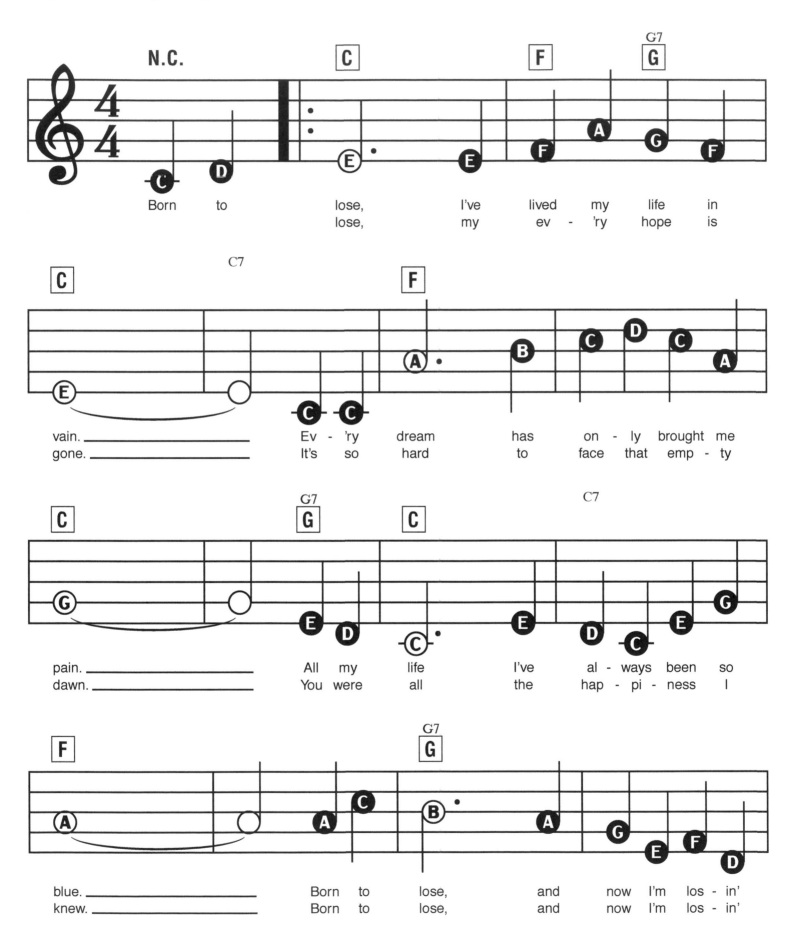

21

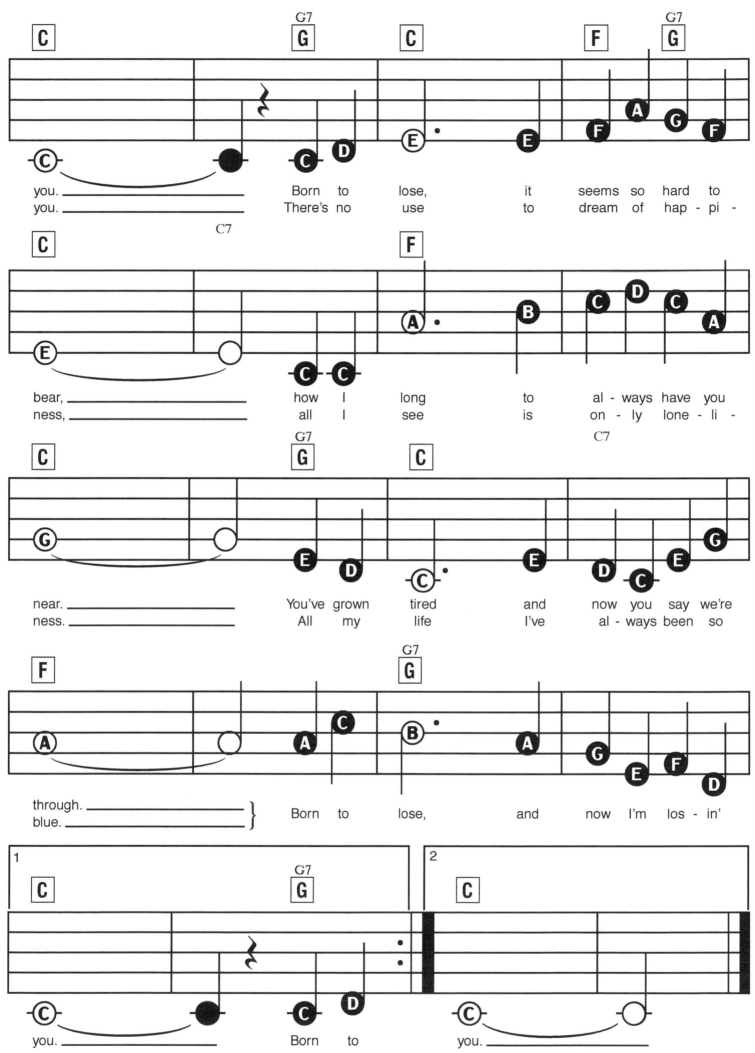

Busted

Registration 4
Rhythm: Country

Words and Music by
Harlan Howard

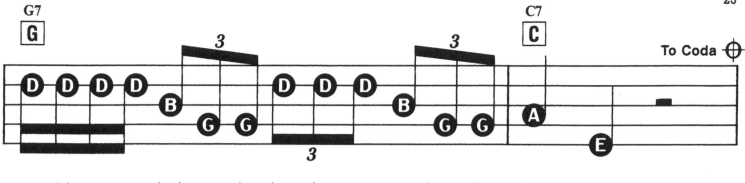

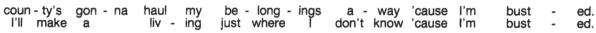

To Coda

count-ty's gon-na haul my be-long-ings a-way 'cause I'm bust - ed.
I'll make a liv-ing just where I don't know 'cause I'm bust - ed.

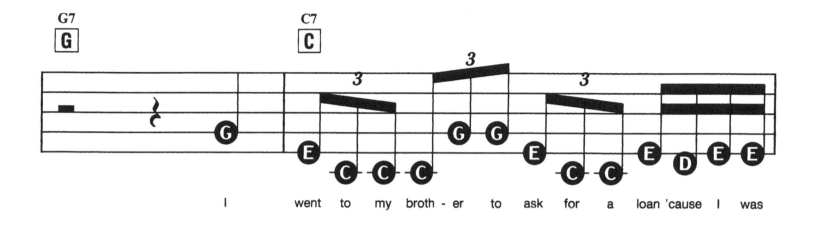

I went to my broth-er to ask for a loan 'cause I was

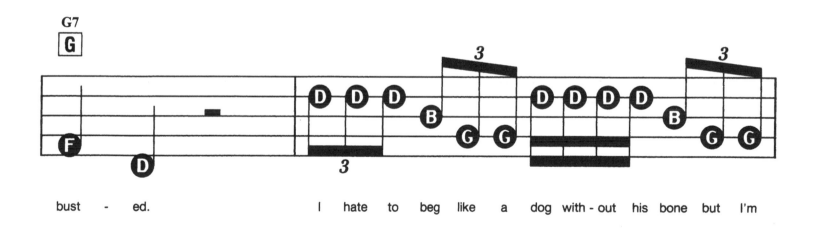

bust - ed. I hate to beg like a dog with-out his bone but I'm

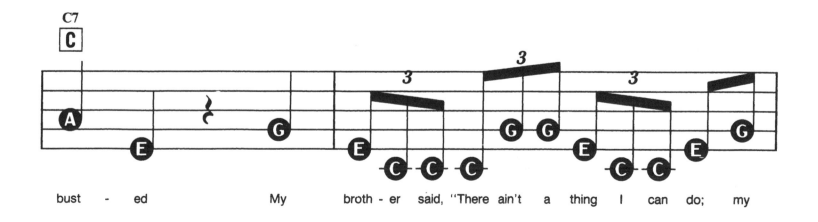

bust - ed My broth-er said, "There ain't a thing I can do; my

24

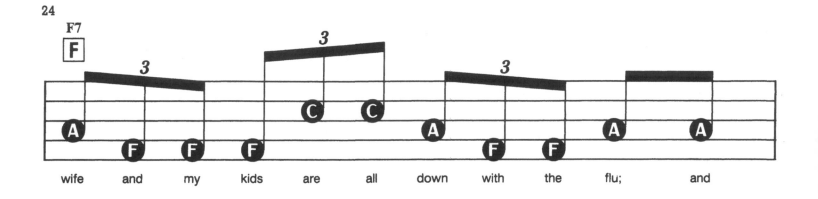

wife   and   my   kids   are   all   down   with   the   flu;   and

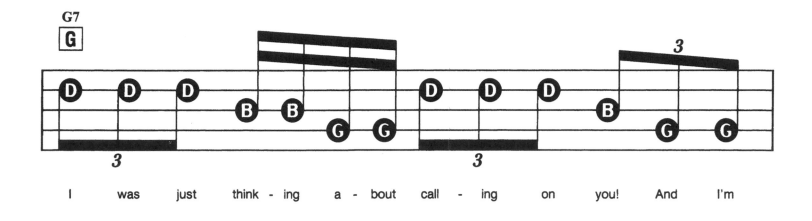

I   was   just   think - ing   a - bout   call - ing   on   you!   And   I'm

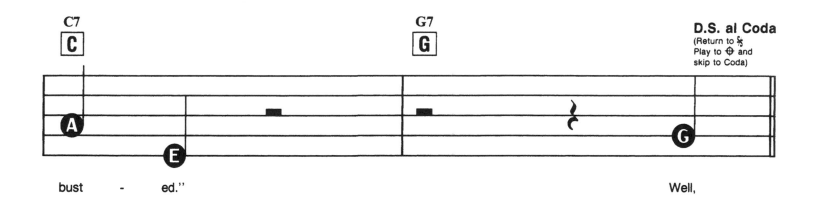

bust - ed."   Well,

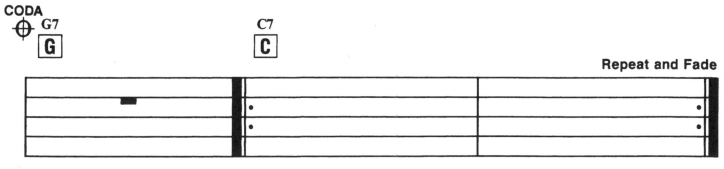

(Spoken:) I'm broke!   *No bread! I mean like nothin' Forget it!*

D-I-V-O-R-C-E

Registration 2
Rhythm: Country

Words and Music by Bobby Braddock
and Curly Putman

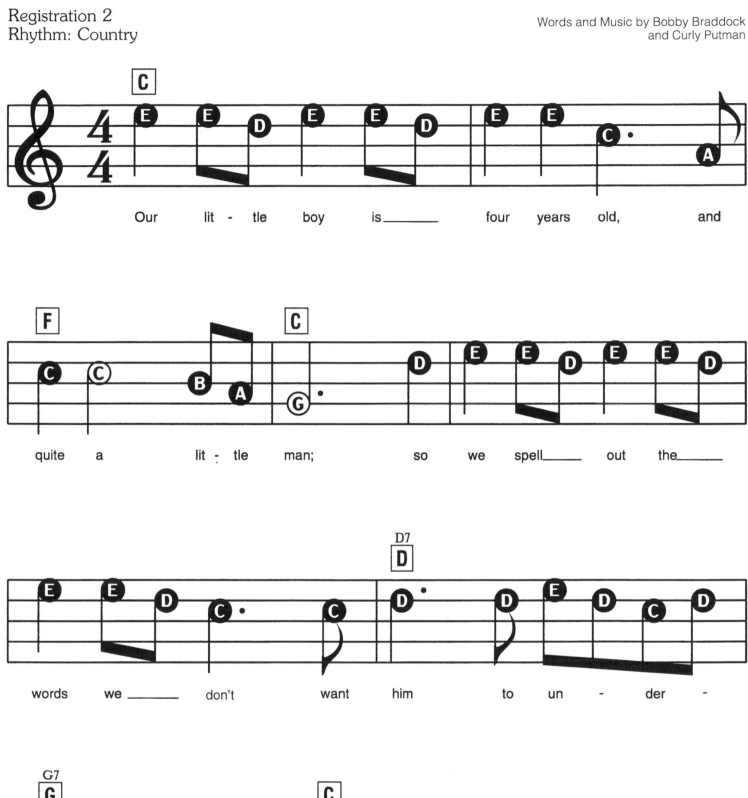

Our lit - tle boy is_____ four years old, and quite a lit - tle man; so we spell_____ out the_____ words we _____ don't want him to un - der - stand. Like T - O - Y or may - be

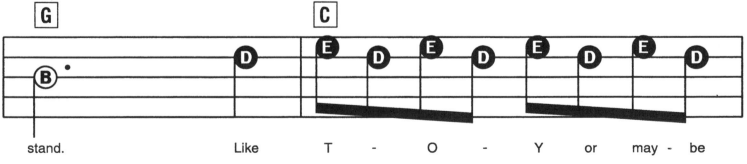

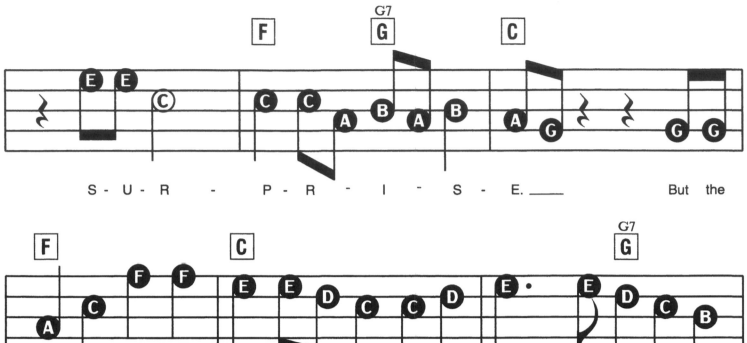

S - U - R - P - R - I - S - E. ____ But the

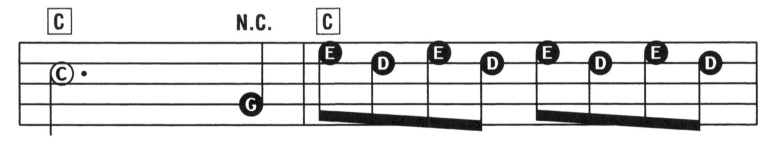

words we're hid - ing from him ____ now tear the heart right out ____ of

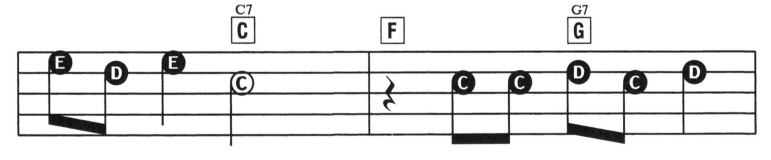

me. Our D - I - V - O -

R - C - E be - comes fi - nal to -

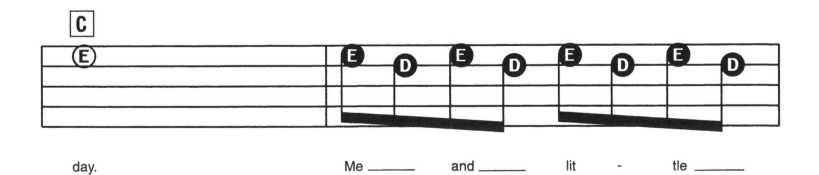

day. Me ____ and ____ lit - tle ____

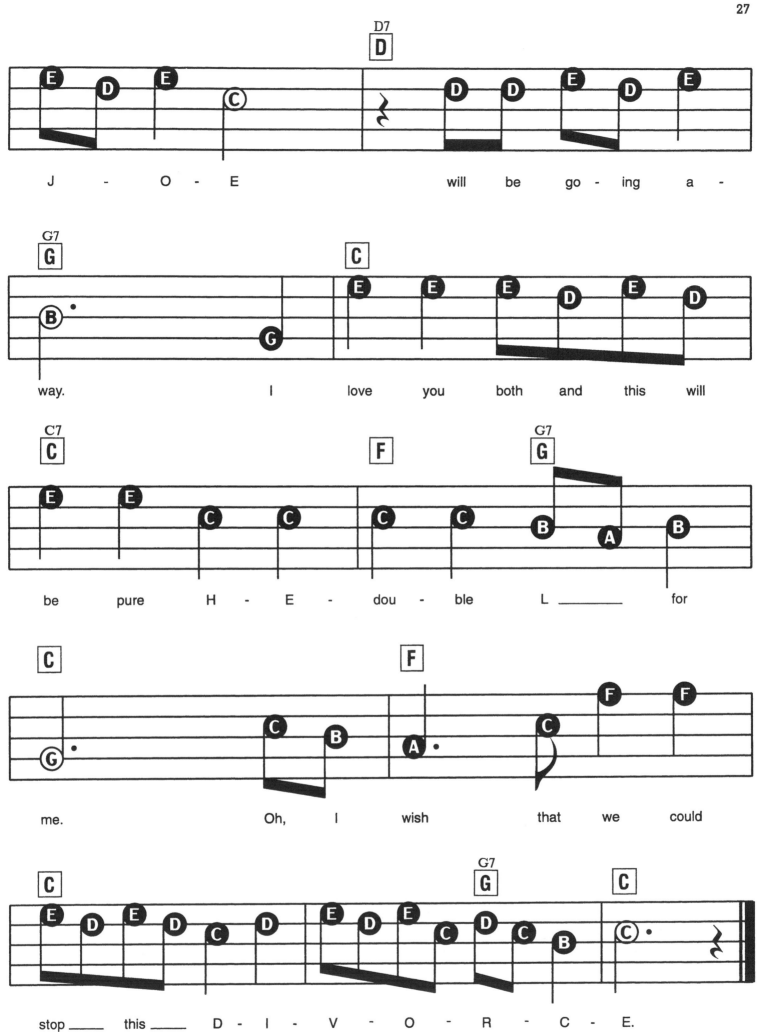

Chattanoogie Shoe Shine Boy

Registration 9
Rhythm: Swing or Big Band

Words and Music by Harry Stone
and Jack Stapp

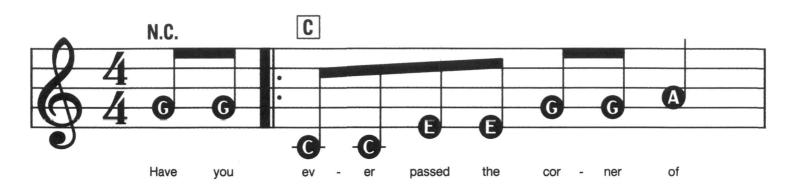

Have you ev - er passed the cor - ner of

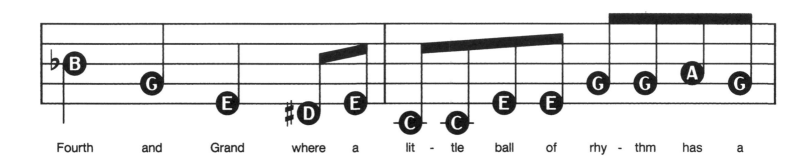

Fourth and Grand where a lit - tle ball of rhy - thm has a

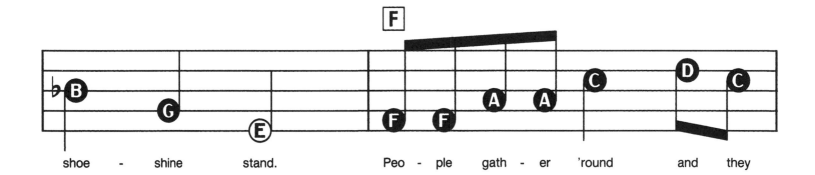

shoe - shine stand. Peo - ple gath - er 'round and they

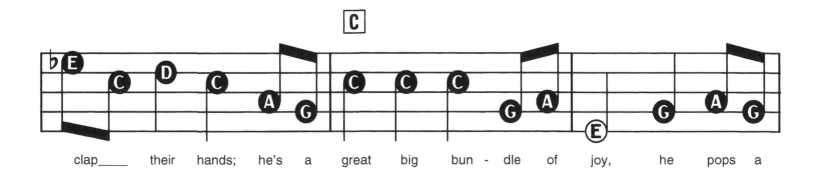

clap____ their hands; he's a great big bun - dle of joy, he pops a

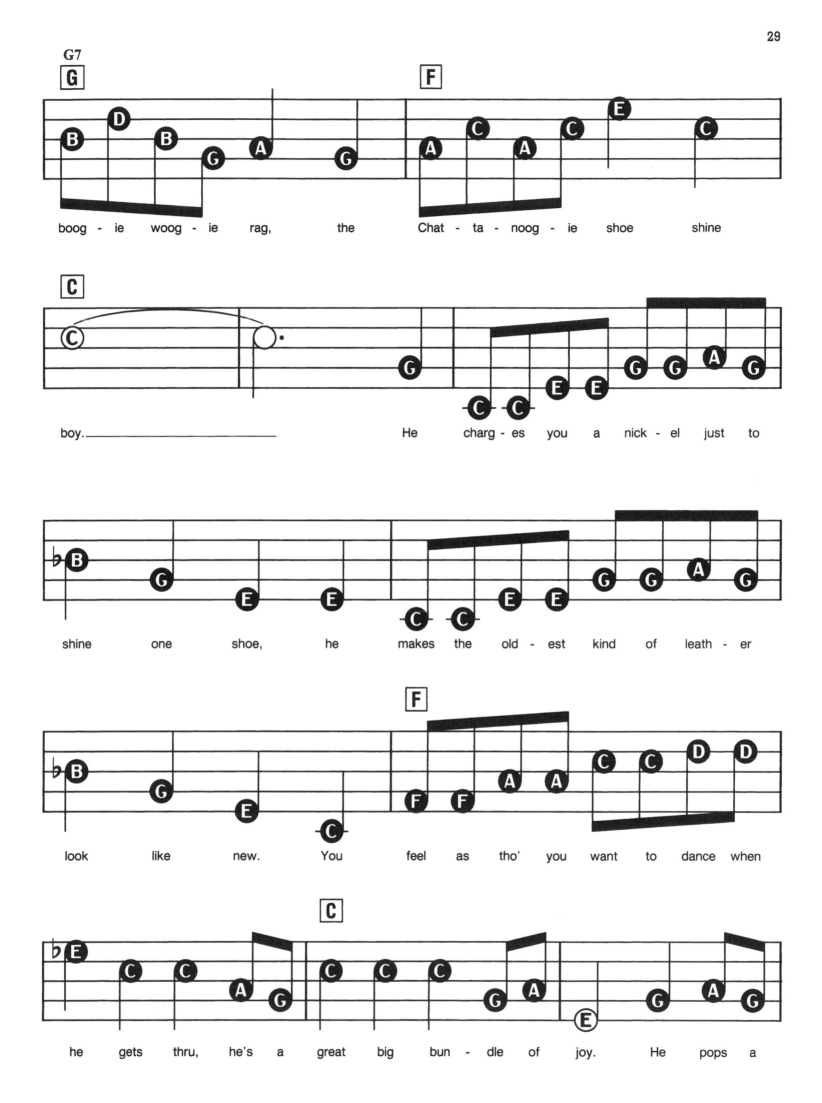

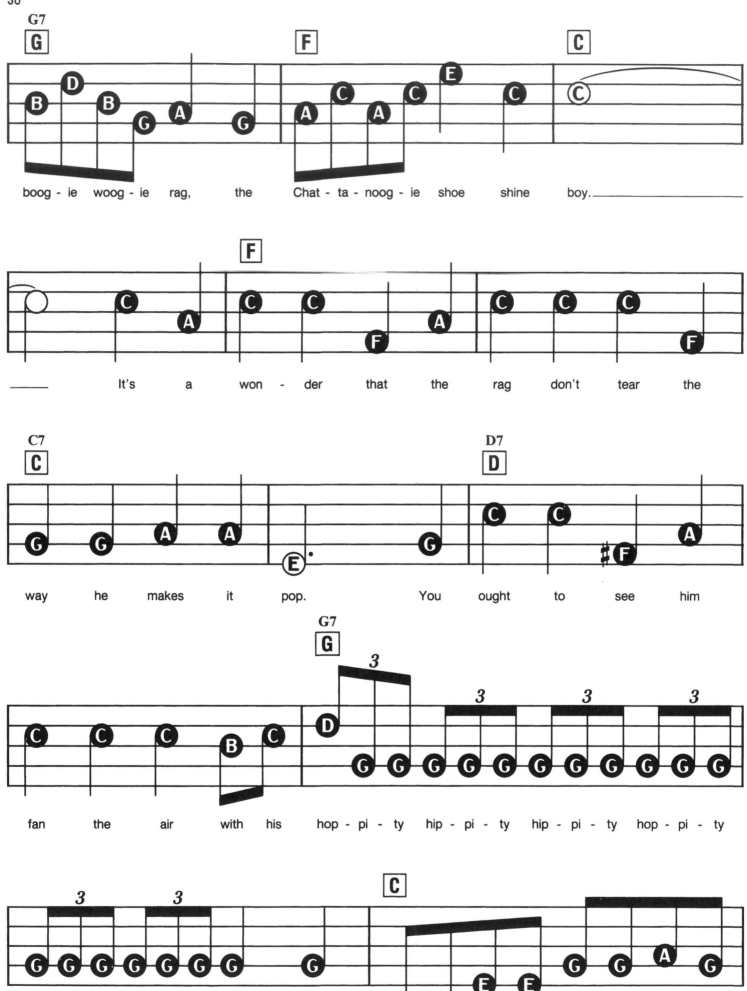

Coat of Many Colors

Registration 2
Rhythm: Country Swing or Fox Trot

Words and Music by
Dolly Parton

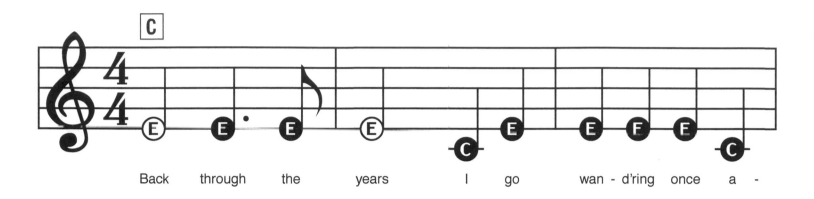

Back through the years I go wan - d'ring once a -

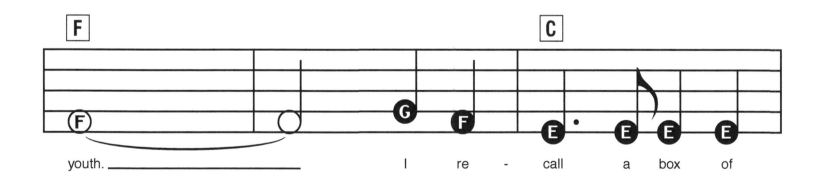

gain, back to the sea - sons of my

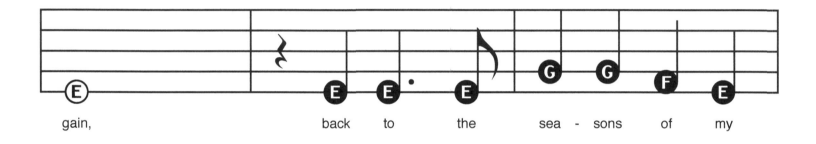

youth. _____ I re - call a box of

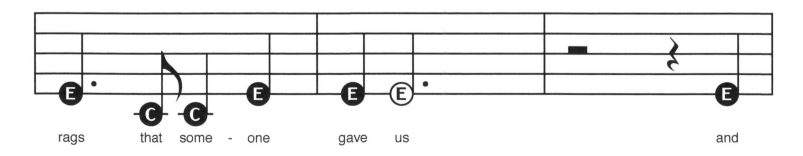

rags that some - one gave us and

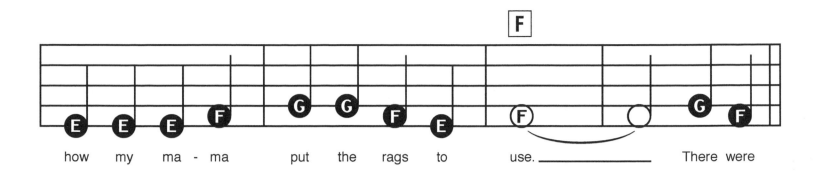

how my ma - ma put the rags to use. _____ There were

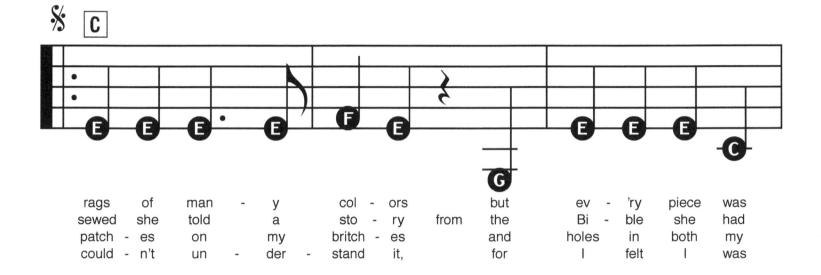

rags of man - y col - ors but ev - 'ry piece was
sewed she told a sto - ry from the Bi - ble she had
patch - es on my britch - es and holes in both my
could - n't un - der - stand it, for I felt I was

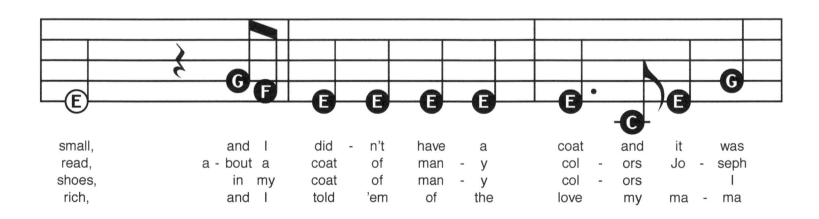

small, and I did - n't have a coat and it was
read, a - bout a coat of man - y col - ors Jo - seph
shoes, in my coat of man - y col - ors I
rich, and I told 'em of the love my ma - ma

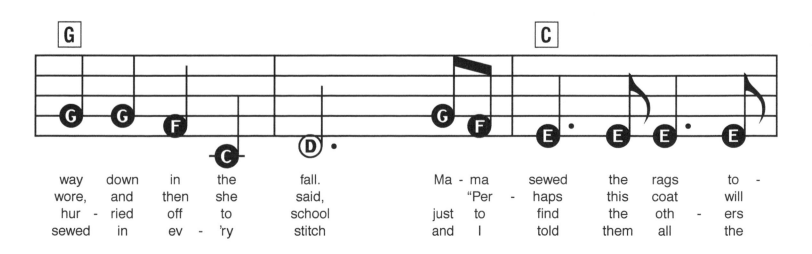

way down in the fall. Ma - ma sewed the rags to -
wore, and then she said, "Per - haps this coat will
hur - ried off to school just to find the oth - ers
sewed in ev - 'ry stitch and I told them all the

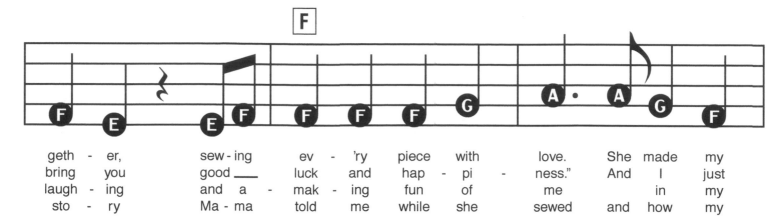

geth - er,	sew - ing	ev - 'ry	piece	with	love.	She	made	my
bring	you	good ___	luck	and	hap - pi -	ness."	And	I	just
laugh - ing	and a -	mak - ing	fun	of	me	in	my
sto - ry	Ma - ma	told	me	while	she	sewed	and	how	my

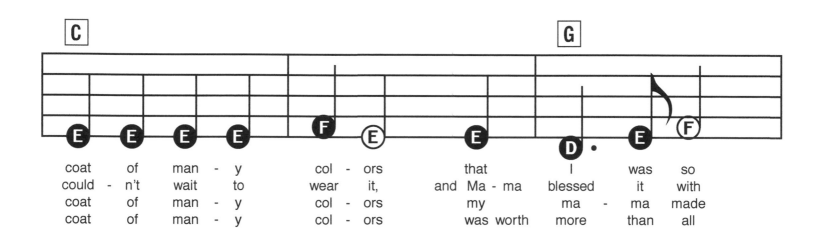

coat	of	man - y	col - ors	that	I	was	so
could - n't	wait	to	wear	it,	and Ma - ma	blessed	it	so	with
coat	of	man - y	col - ors	my	ma - ma	made
coat	of	man - y	col - ors	was worth	more	than	all

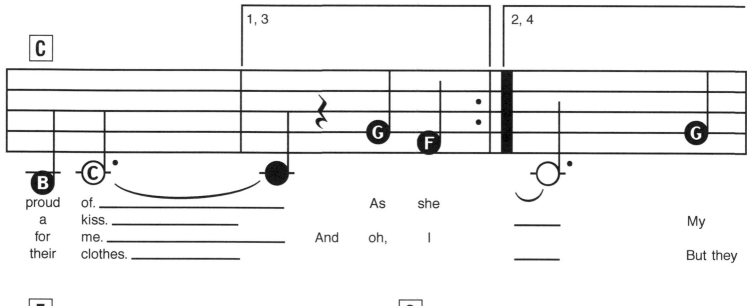

proud	of. ___	As	she
a	kiss. ___	And	oh,	I
for	me. ___	My
their	clothes. ___	But they

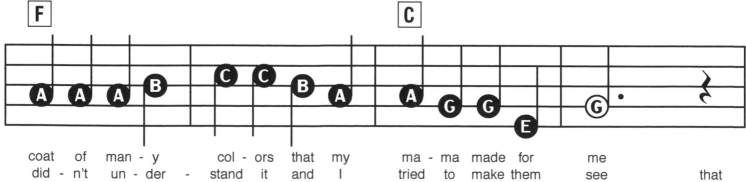

| coat | of | man - y | col - ors | that | my | ma - ma | made | for | me |
| did - n't | un - der - | stand | it | and | I | tried | to | make | them | see | that |

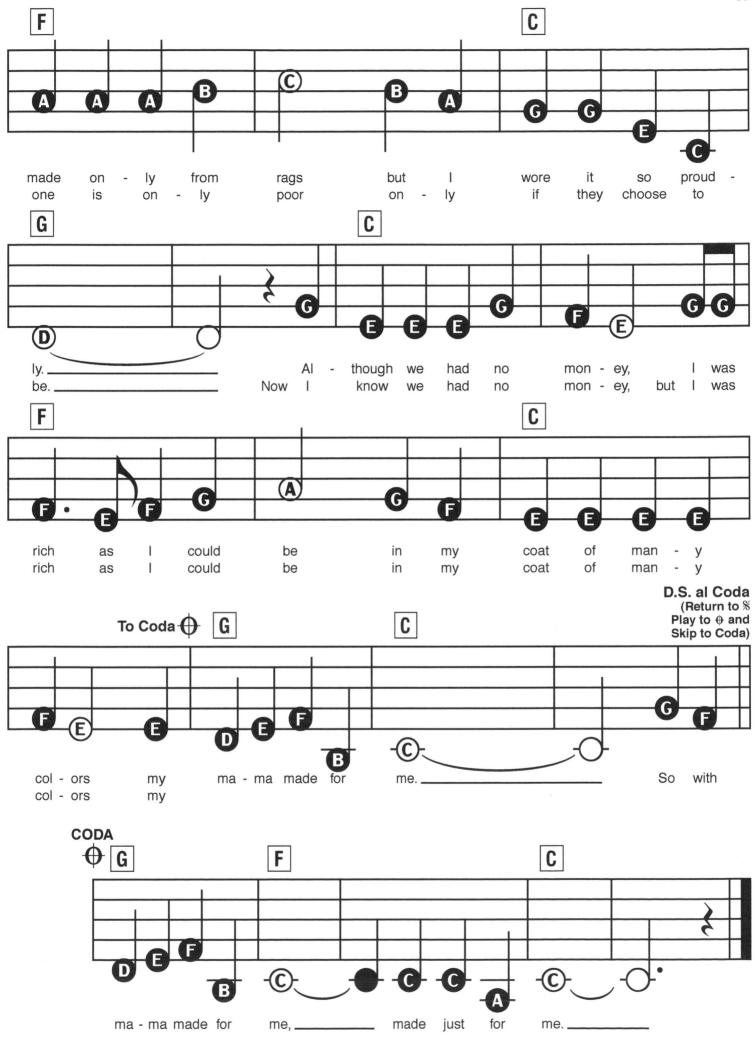

Cold, Cold Heart

Registration 4
Rhythm: Country or Fox Trot

Words and Music by
Hank Williams

I've tried so hard, my dear, to show that
oth - er love be - fore my time that made
was a time when I be - lieved that

you're my ev - 'ry dream, yet
your heart sad and blue, and
you be - longed to me, but

you're a - fraid each thing I do is just some e - vil
so my heart is pay - ing now for things I did - n't
now I know your heart is shack - led to a mem - o -

scheme. A mem - 'ry from your lone - some past
do. In an - ger, un - kind words I said
ry. The more I learn to care for you, the

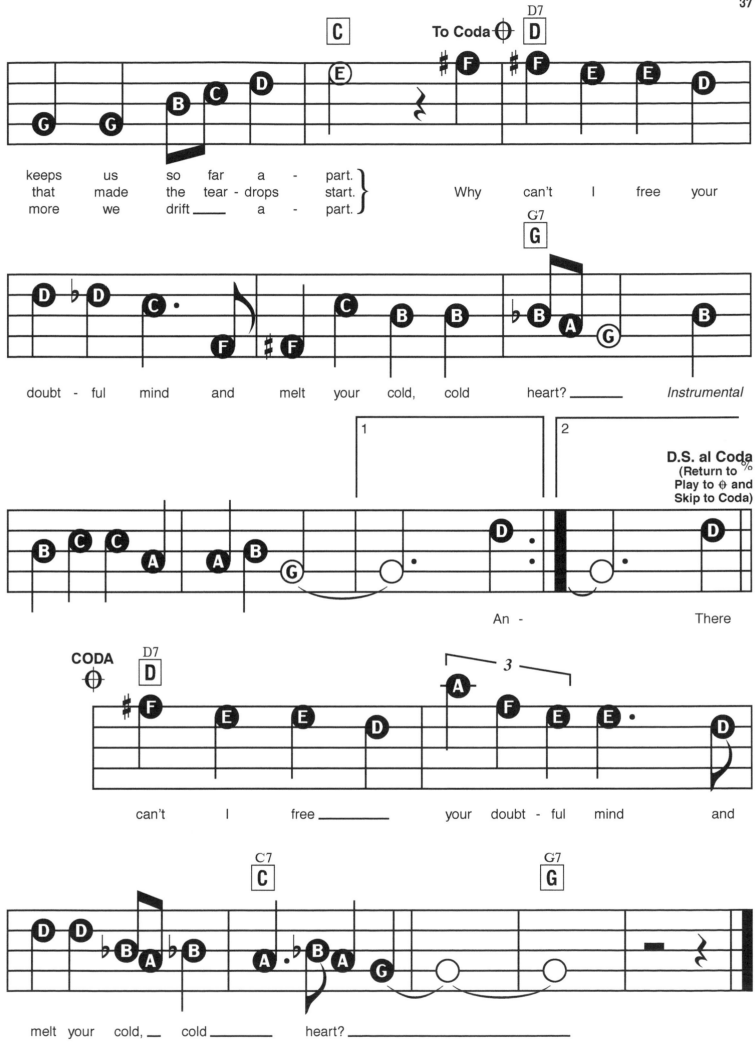

Cryin' Time

Registration 3
Rhythm: Country

Words and Music by
Buck Owens

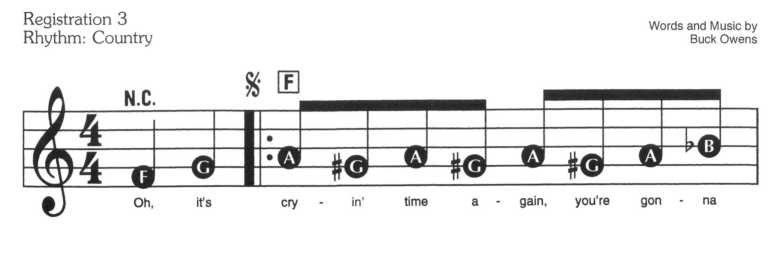

Oh, it's cry - in' time a - gain, you're gon - na

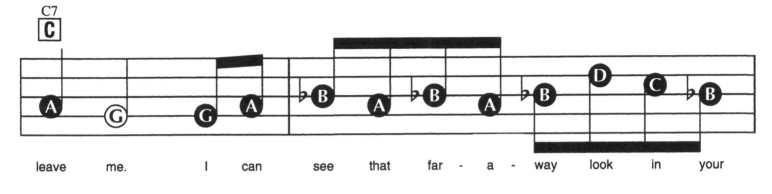

leave me. I can see that far - a - way look in your

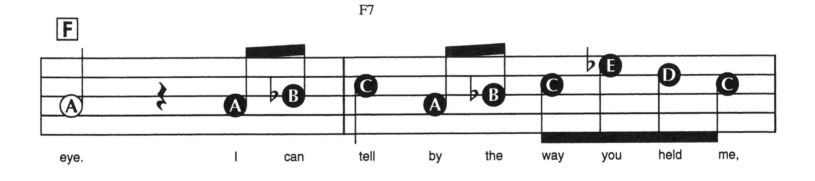

eye. I can tell by the way you held me,

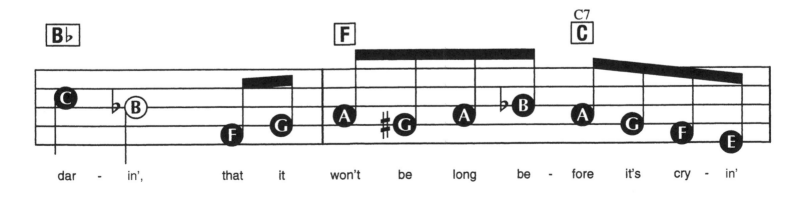

dar - in', that it won't be long be - fore it's cry - in'

Deep in the Heart of Texas

Registration 2
Rhythm: Country Swing or Western

Words by June Hershey
Music by Don Swander

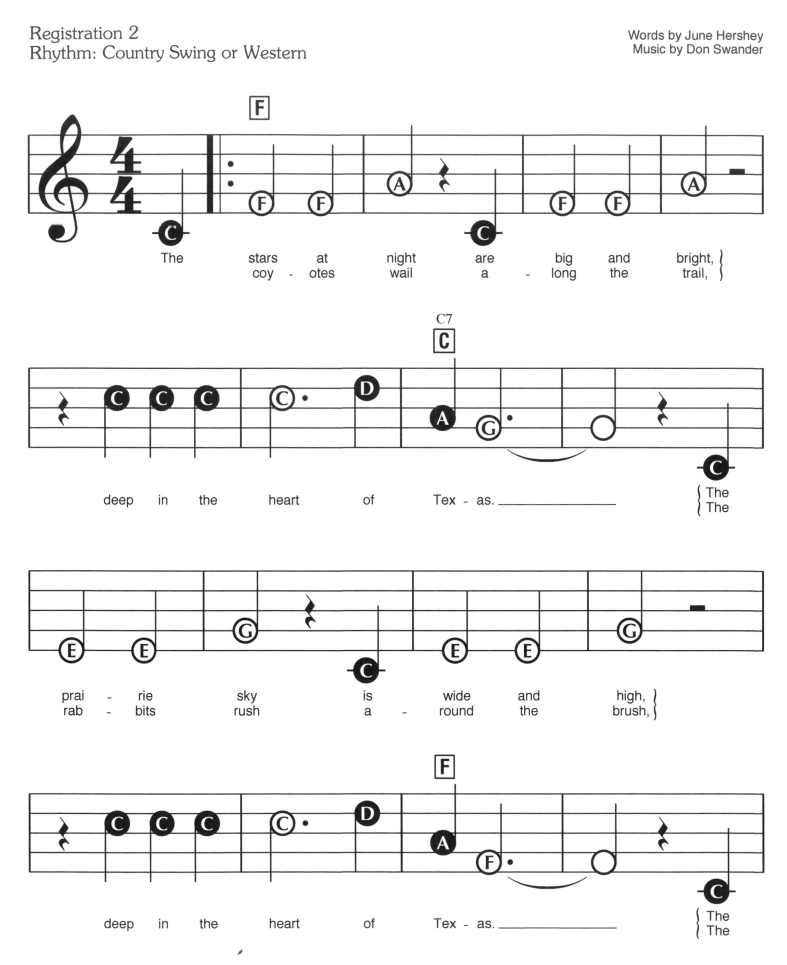

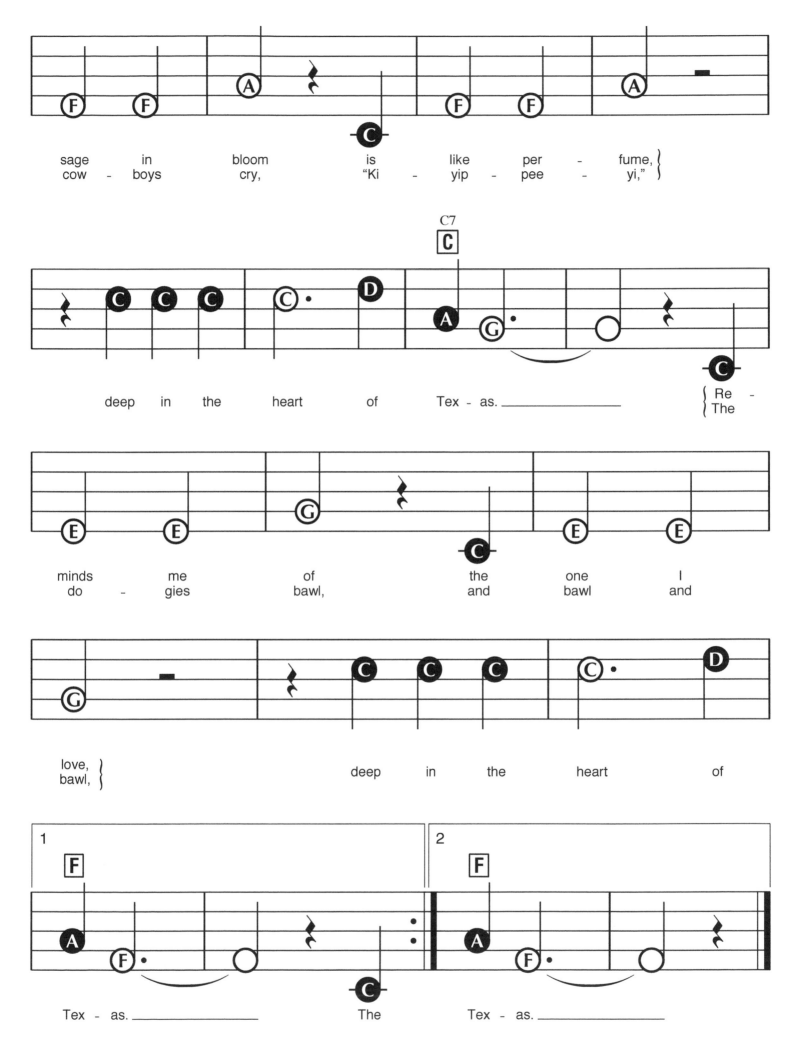

The Devil Went Down to Georgia

Registration 4
Rhythm: Country Swing or Fox Trot

Words and Music by Charlie Daniels,
John Thomas Crain, Jr., William Joel DiGregorio, Fred Laroy Edwards,
Charles Fred Hayward and James Wainwright Marshall

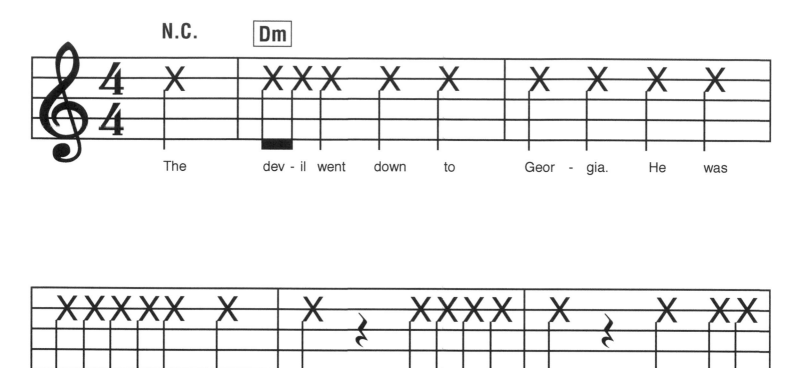

The dev - il went down to Geor - gia. He was

look-in' for a soul to steal. He was in a bind 'cause he was

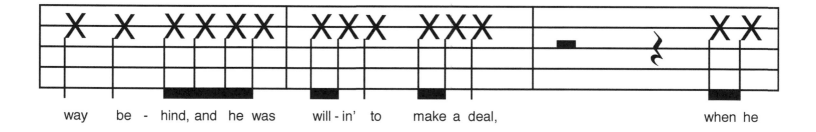

way be - hind, and he was will - in' to make a deal, when he

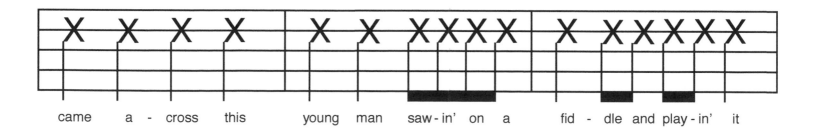

came a - cross this young man saw-in' on a fid - dle and play-in' it

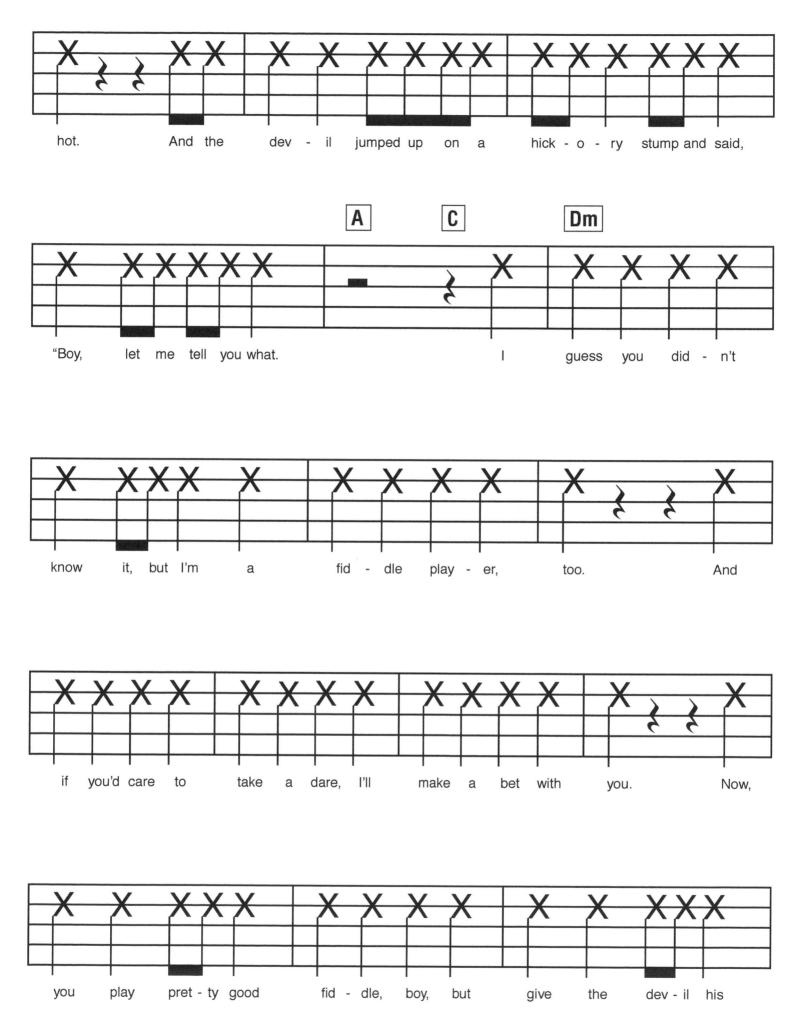

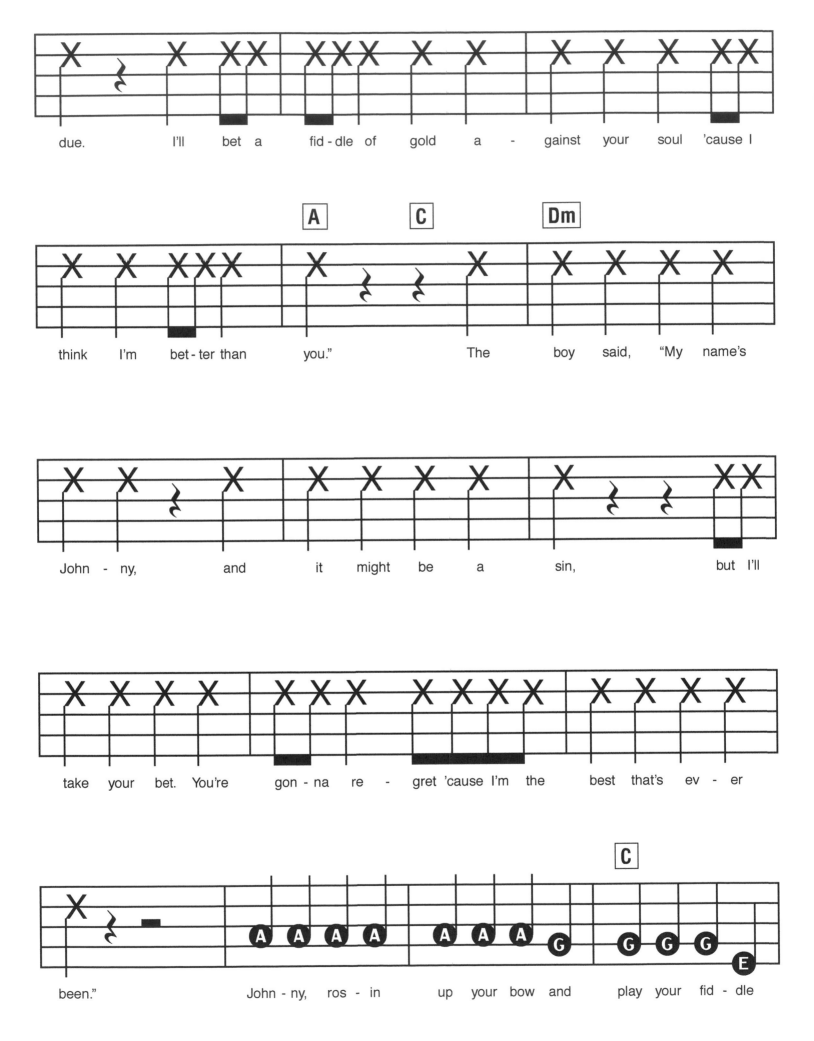

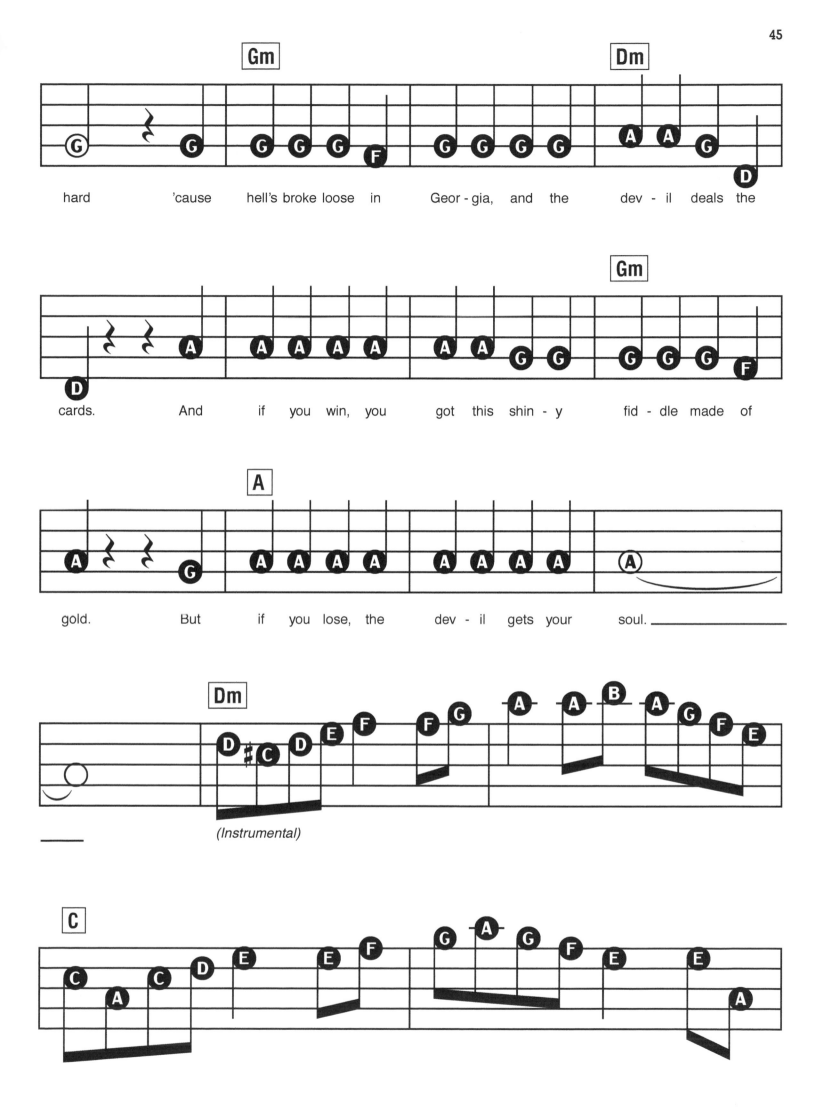

hard 'cause hell's broke loose in Geor - gia, and the dev - il deals the

cards. And if you win, you got this shin - y fid - dle made of

gold. But if you lose, the dev - il gets your soul. _____

_____ *(Instrumental)*

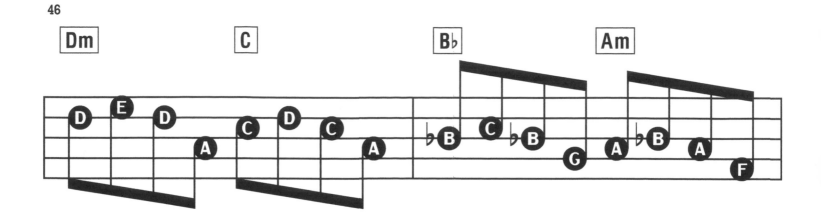

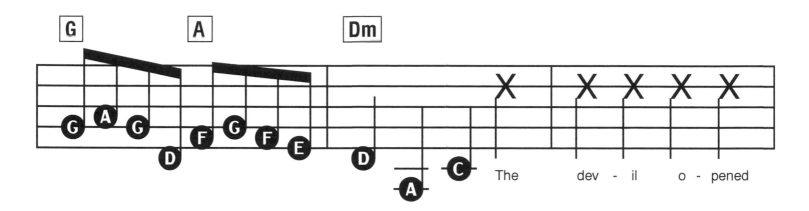

The dev - il o - pened

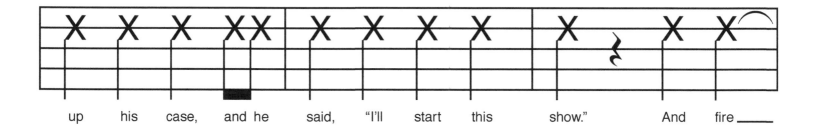

up his case, and he said, "I'll start this show." And fire____

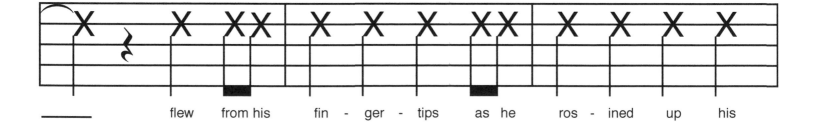

____ flew from his fin - ger - tips as he ros - ined up his

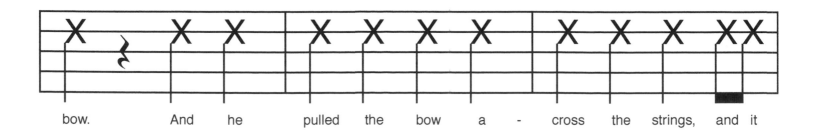

bow. And he pulled the bow a - cross the strings, and it

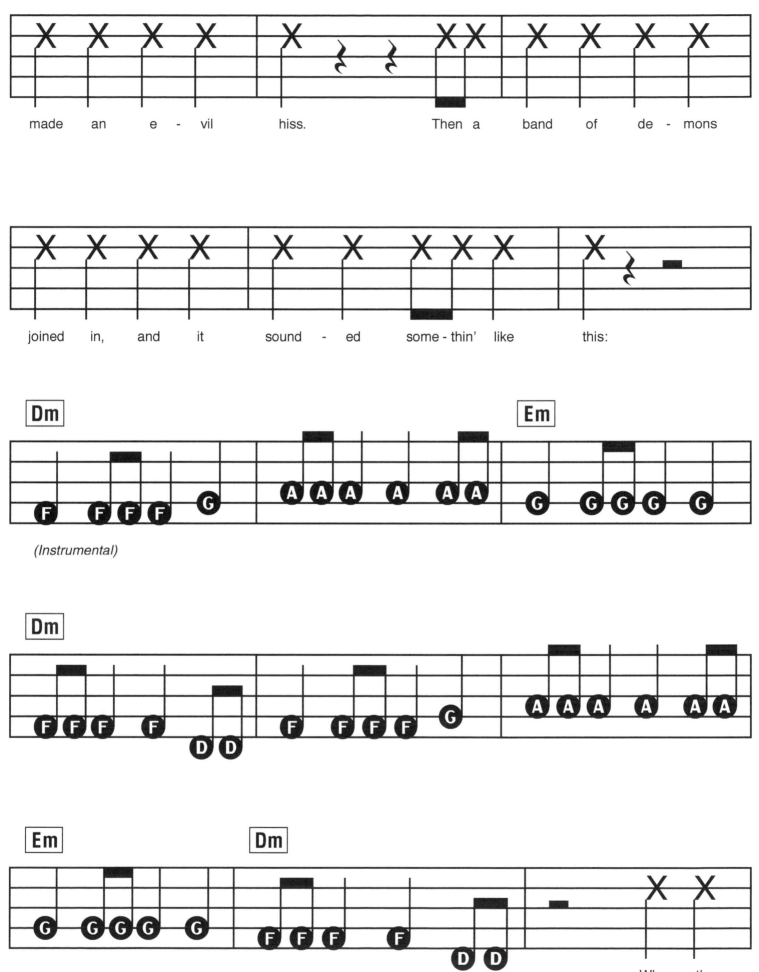

made an e - vil hiss. Then a band of de - mons

joined in, and it sound - ed some - thin' like this:

(Instrumental)

When the

48

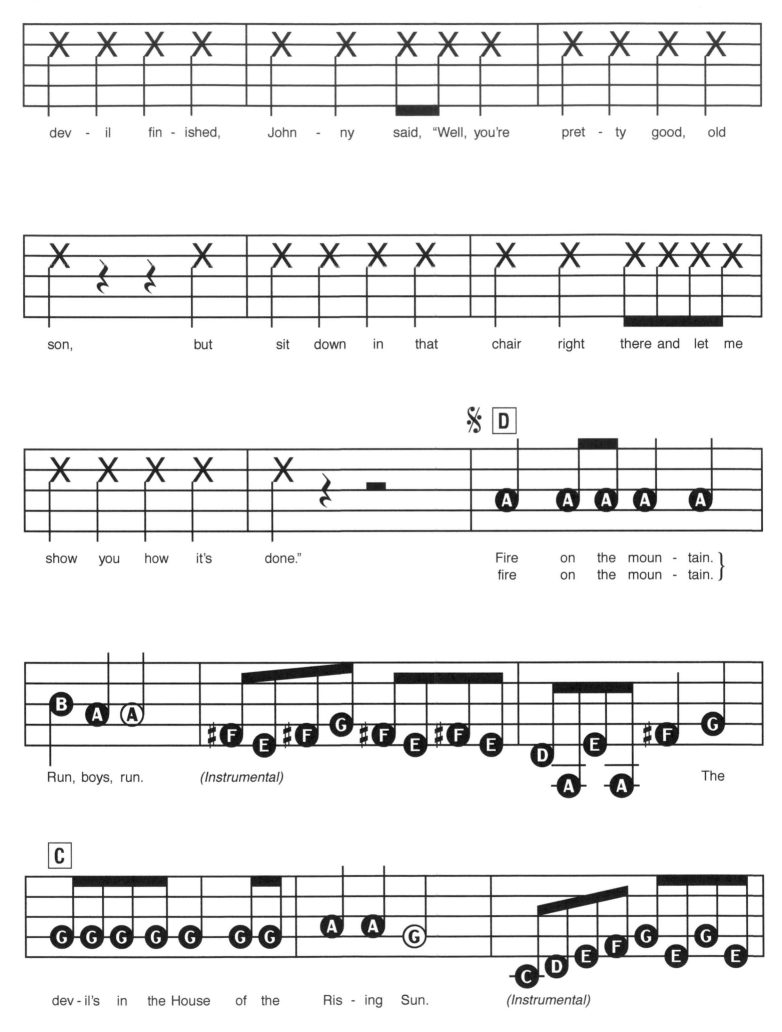

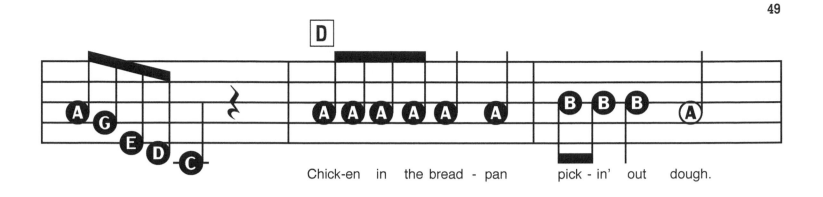

Chick-en in the bread - pan pick - in' out dough.

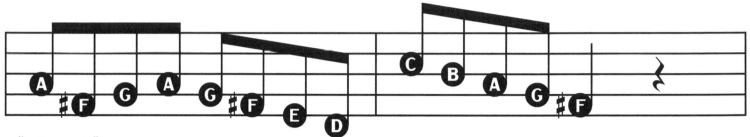

(Instrumental)

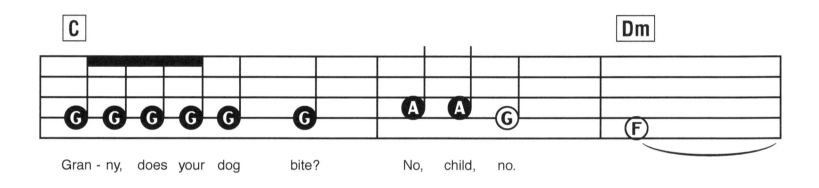

Gran - ny, does your dog bite? No, child, no.

To Coda ⊕

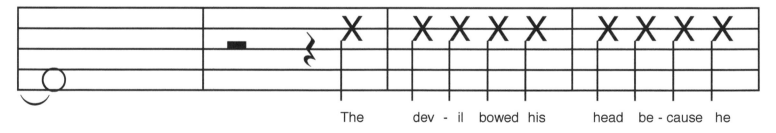

The dev - il bowed his head be - cause he

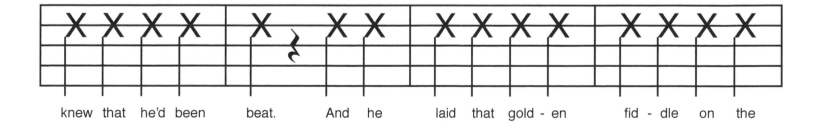

knew that he'd been beat. And he laid that gold - en fid - dle on the

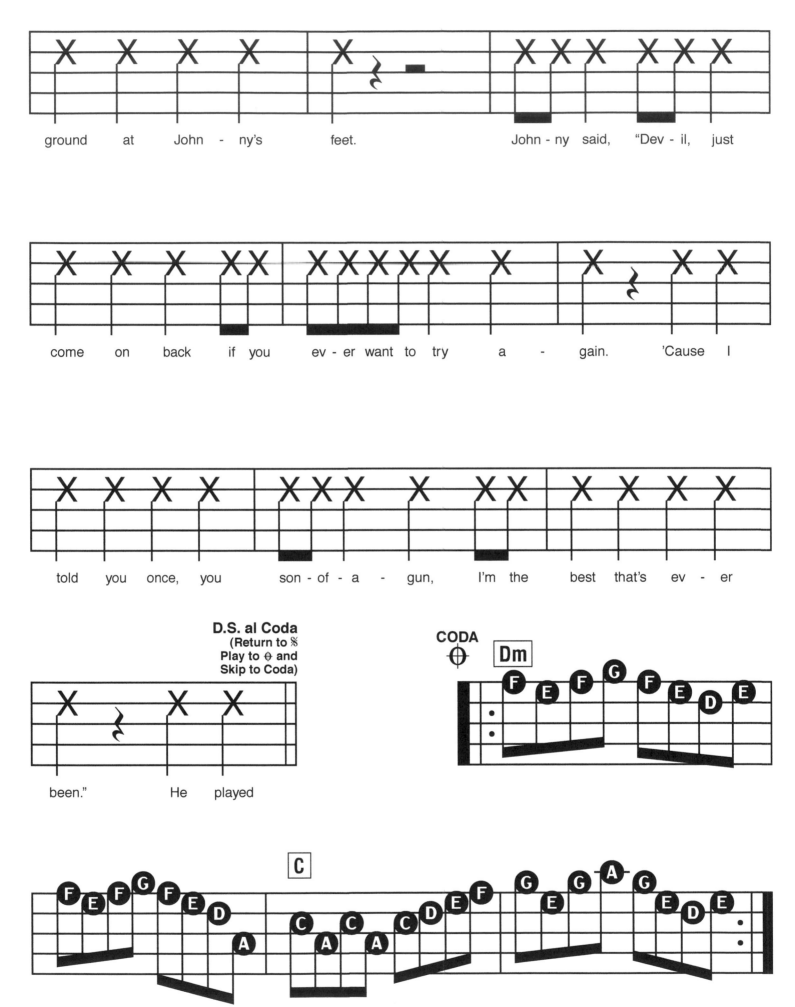

ground at John - ny's feet. John - ny said, "Dev - il, just

come on back if you ev - er want to try a - gain. 'Cause I

told you once, you son - of - a - gun, I'm the best that's ev - er

D.S. al Coda
(Return to %
Play to ⊕ and
Skip to Coda)

been." He played

CODA
⊕

Dm

C

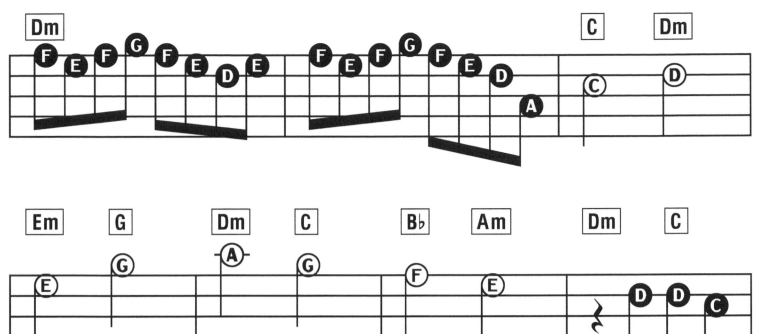

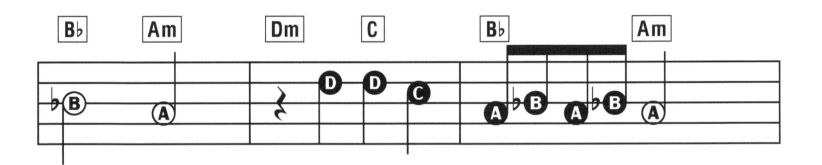

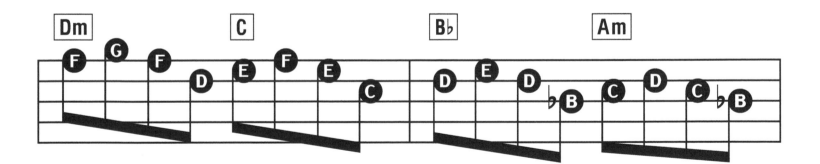

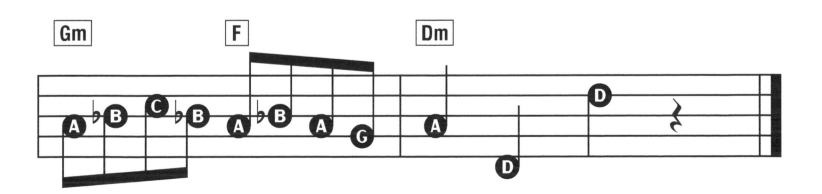

Down at the Twist and Shout

Registration 1
Rhythm: Country or Polka

Words and Music by
Mary Chapin Carpenter

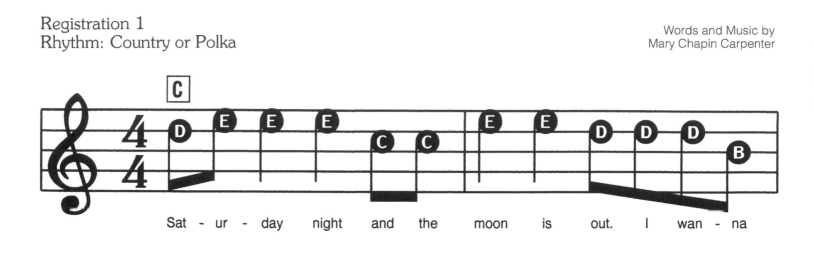

Sat - ur - day night and the moon is out. I wan - na

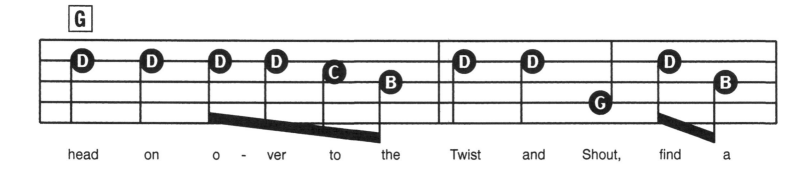

head on o - ver to the Twist and Shout, find a

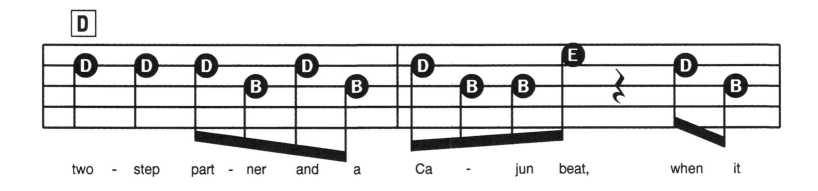

two - step part - ner and a Ca - jun beat, when it

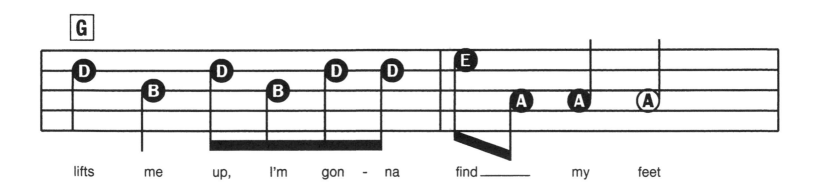

lifts me up, I'm gon - na find_____ my feet

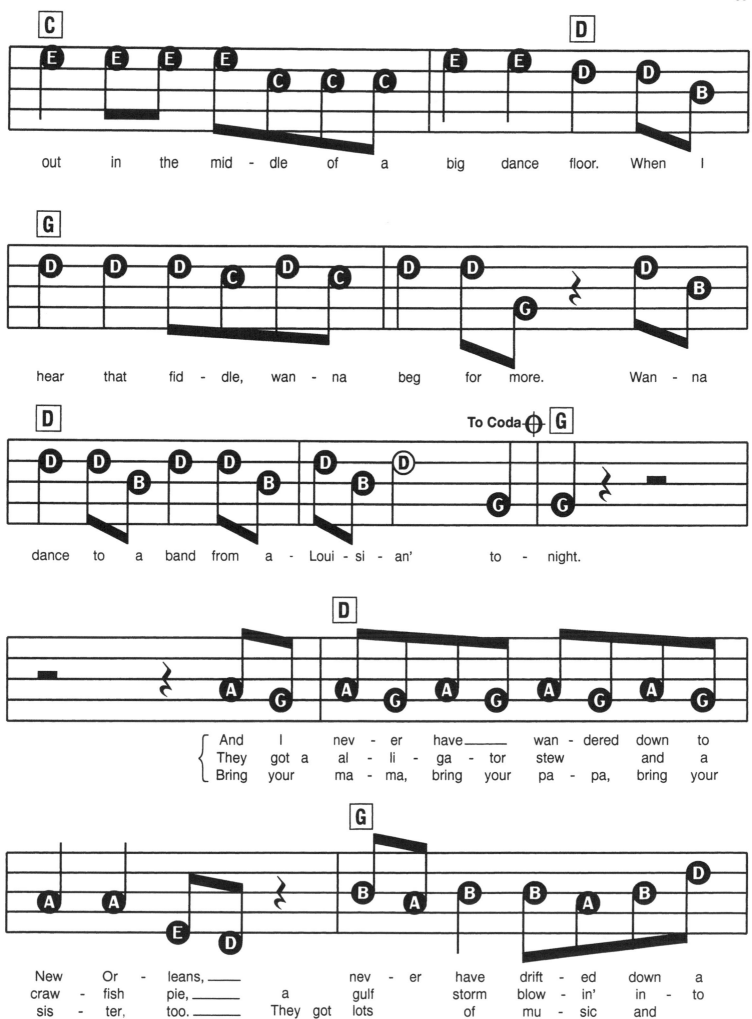

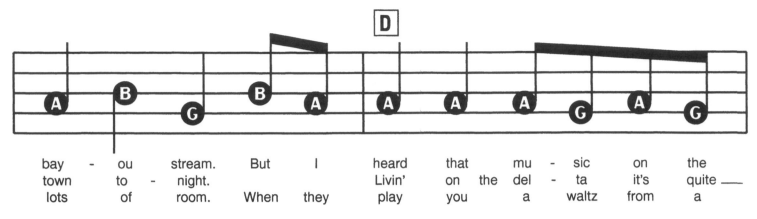

bay - ou stream. But I heard that mu - sic on the
town to - night. Livin' on the del - ta it's quite ___
lots of room. When they play you a waltz from a

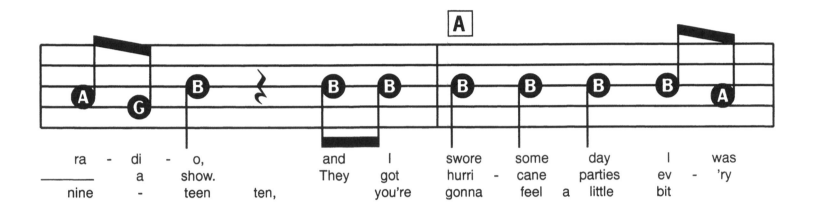

ra - di - o, and I swore some day I was
___ a show. They got hurri - cane parties ev - 'ry
nine - teen ten, you're gonna feel a little bit

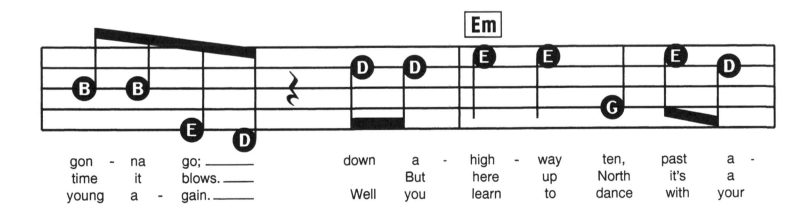

gon - na go; ___ down a - high - way ten, past a -
time it blows. ___ But here up North it's a
young a - gain. ___ Well you learn to dance with your

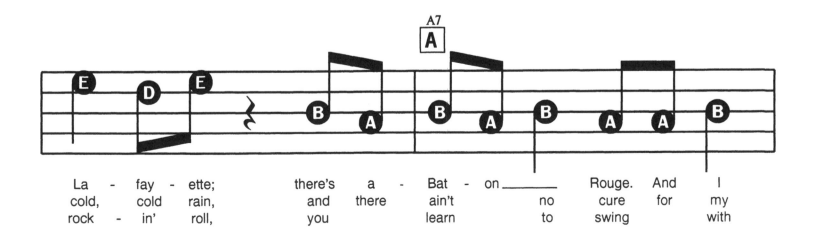

La - fay - ette; there's a - Bat - on ___ Rouge. And I
cold, cold rain, and there ain't no cure for my
rock - in' roll, you learn to swing with

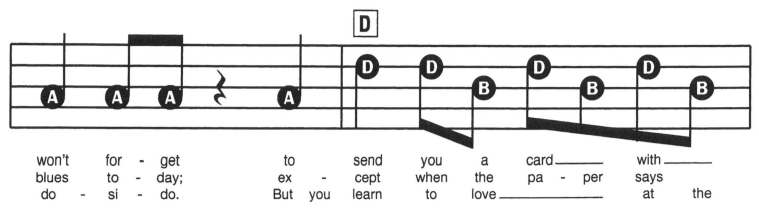

won't for - get | to send you a card_____ with _____
blues to - day; | ex - cept when the pa - per says
do - si - do. | But you learn to love_____ at the

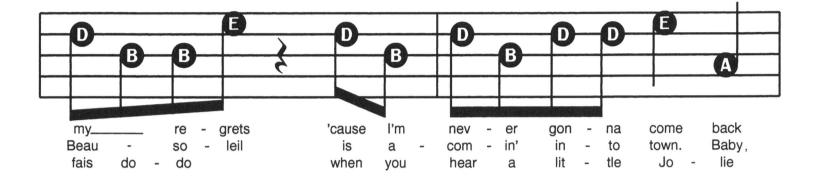

my_____ re - grets | 'cause I'm nev - er gon - na come back
Beau - so - leil | is a - com - in' in - to town. Baby,
fais do - do | when you hear a lit - tle Jo - lie

1,2 | **3**

D.C. al Coda
(Return to beginning
Play to ⊕ and
Skip to Coda)

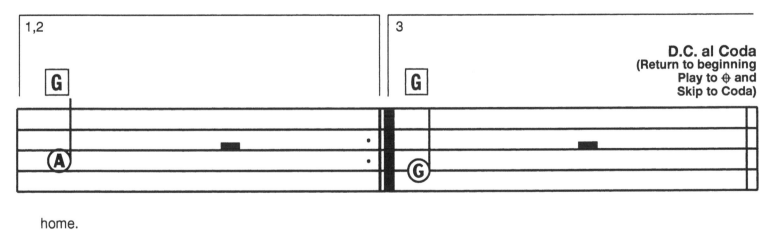

home.
let's go down. It's Blon.

CODA ⊕

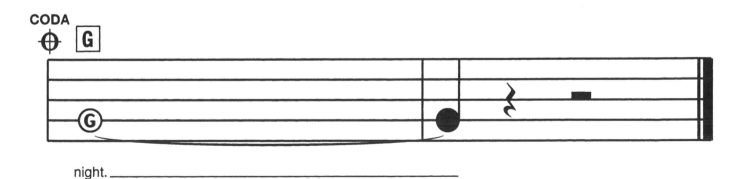

night. _____
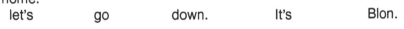

El Paso

Registration 5
Rhythm: Waltz

Words and Music by
Marty Robbins

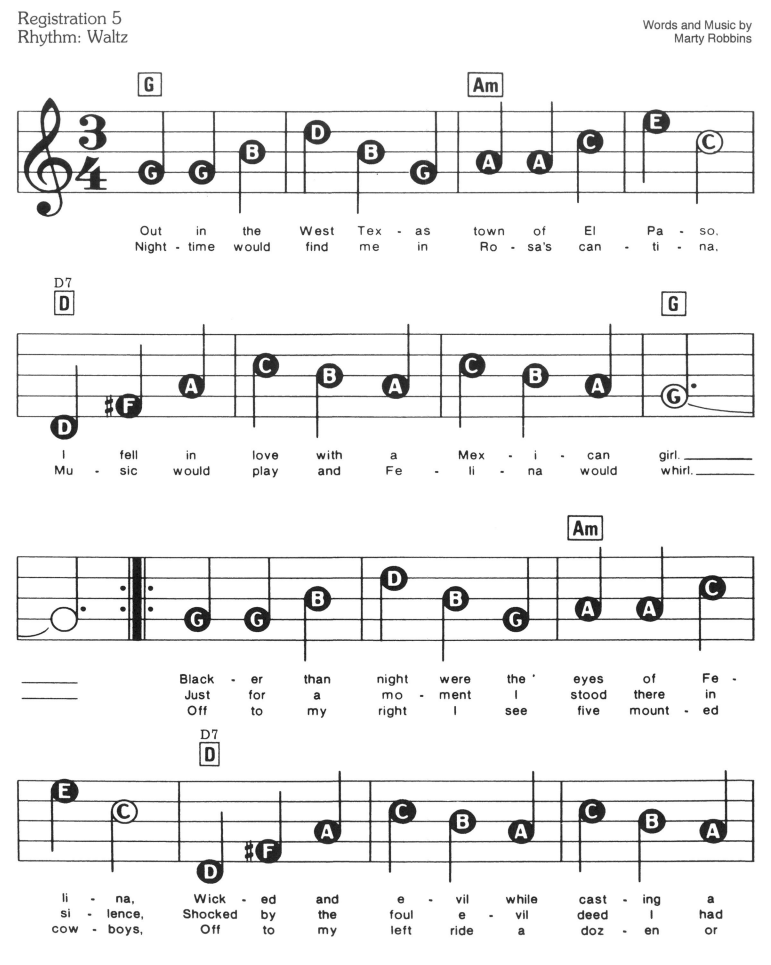

Out in the West Tex - as town of El Pa - so,
Night - time would find me in Ro - sa's can - ti - na,

I fell in love with a Mex - i - can girl. _____
Mu - sic would play and a Fe - li - na would whirl. _____

_____ Black - er than night were the eyes of Fe -
Just for a mo - ment I stood there in
Off to my right I see five mount - ed

li - na, Wick - ed and e - vil while cast - ing a
si - lence, Shocked by the foul e - vil deed I had
cow - boys, Off to my left ride a doz - en or

57

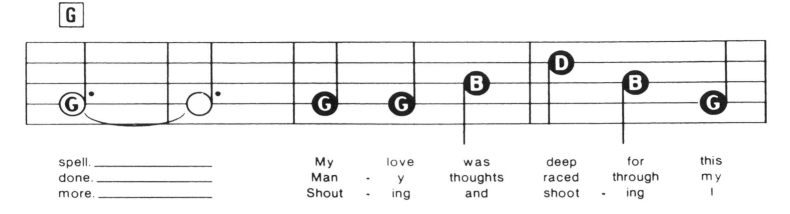

spell. _____
done. _____
more. _____

My   love   was   deep   for   this
Man - y   thoughts   raced   through   my
Shout - ing   and   shoot - ing   I

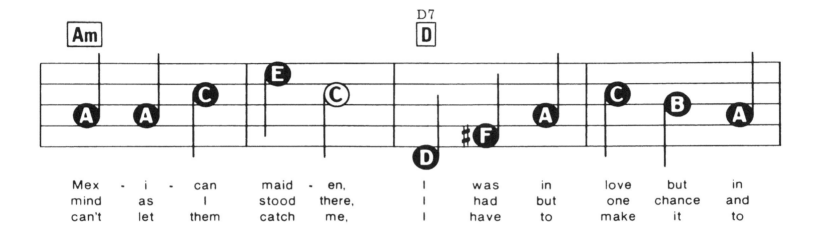

Mex - i - can   maid - en,   I   was   in   love   but   in
mind   as   I   stood   there,   I   had   but   one   chance   and
can't   let   them   catch   me,   I   have   to   make   it   to

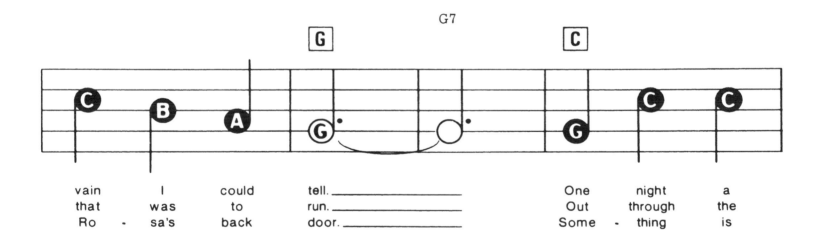

vain   I   could   tell. _____   One   night   a
that   I   was   to   run. _____   Out   through   the
Ro - sa's   back   door. _____   Some - thing   is

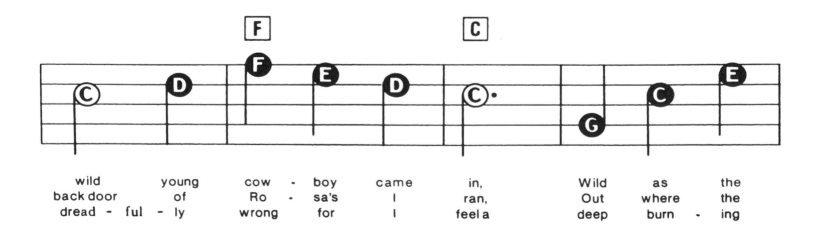

wild   young   cow - boy   came   in,   Wild   as   the
back door   of   Ro - sa's   I   ran,   Out   where   the
dread - ful - ly   wrong   for   I   feel a   deep   burn - ing

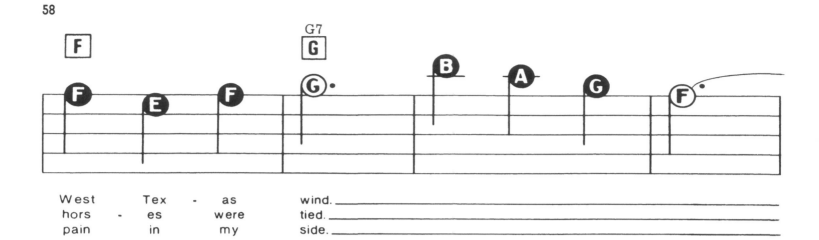

West   Tex - as   wind. _____
hors - es   were   tied. _____
pain   in   my   side. _____

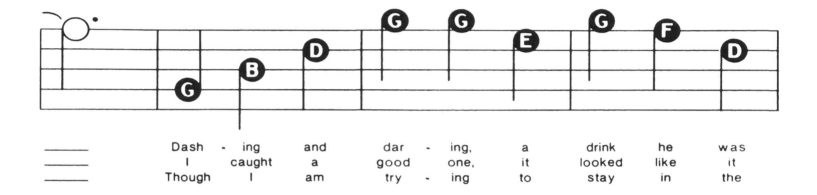

_____   Dash - ing   and   dar - ing,   a   drink   he   was
_____   I   caught   a   good   one,   it   looked   like   it
_____   Though   I   am   try - ing   to   stay   in   the

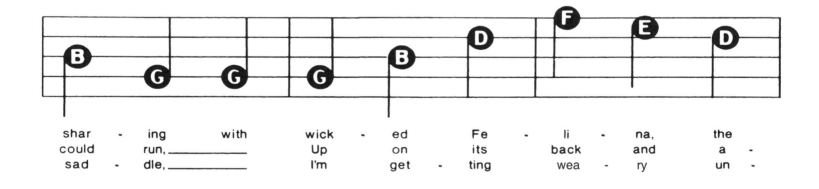

shar - ing   with   wick - ed   Fe - li - na,   the
could   run, _____   Up   on   its   back   and   a -
sad - dle, _____   I'm   get - ting   wea - ry   un -

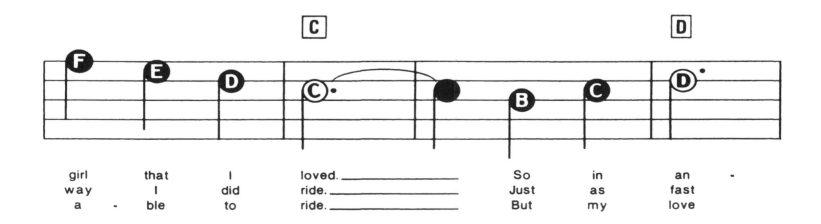

girl   that   I   loved. _____   So   in   an -
way   I   did   ride. _____   Just   as   fast
a - ble   to   ride. _____   But   my   love

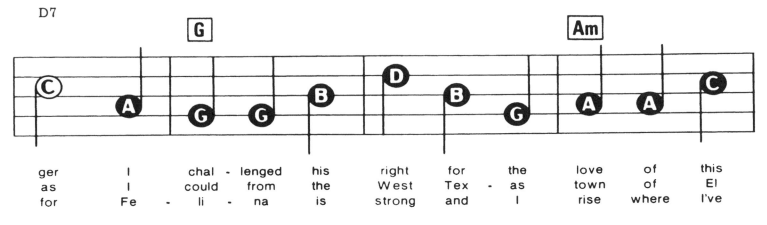

ger   I   chal - lenged his   right   for   the   love   of   this
as   I   could   from the   West   Tex   -   as   town   of   El
for   Fe - li -   na   is   strong   and   I   rise   where   I've

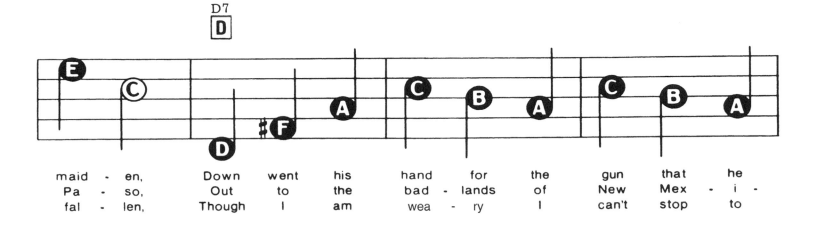

maid - en,   Down went   his   hand   for   the   gun   that   he
Pa - so,   Out to   the   bad - lands of   New   Mex - i -
fal - len,   Though I   am   wea - ry I   can't   stop   to

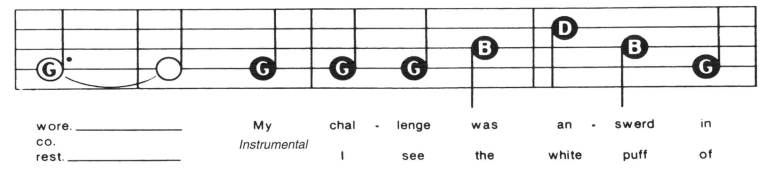

wore. _____   My   chal - lenge was   an - swerd in
co.   *Instrumental*   I   see   the   white   puff   of
rest. _____   I   feel   the   bul - let   go

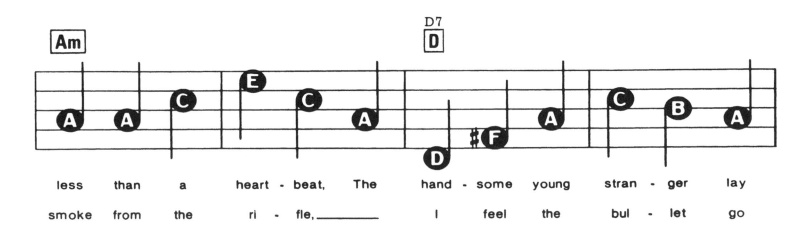

less   than   a   heart - beat, The   hand - some young   stran - ger lay
smoke   from   the   ri - fle, _____ I   feel   the   bul - let go

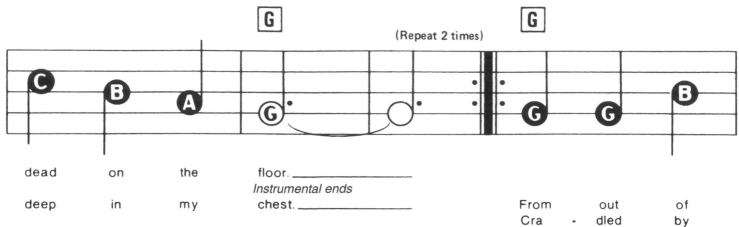

dead   on   the   floor._____

Instrumental ends

deep   in   my   chest._____   From   out   of

Cra - dled by

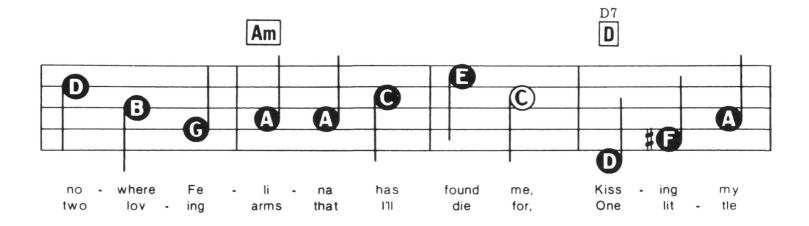

no - where   Fe - li - na   has   found   me,   Kiss - ing   my

two   lov - ing   arms   that   I'll   die   for,   One   lit - tle

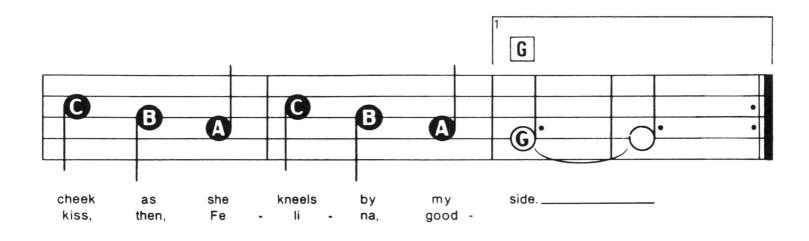

cheek   as   she   kneels   by   my   side._____

kiss,   then,   Fe - li - na,   good -

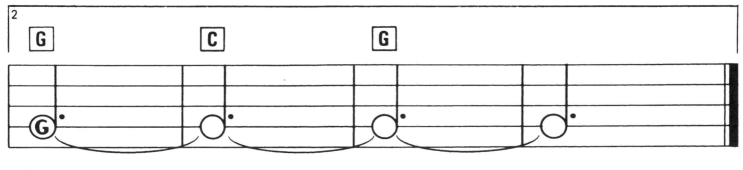

bye._____

Elvira

Registration 4
Rhythm: Country or March

Words and Music by
Dallas Frazier

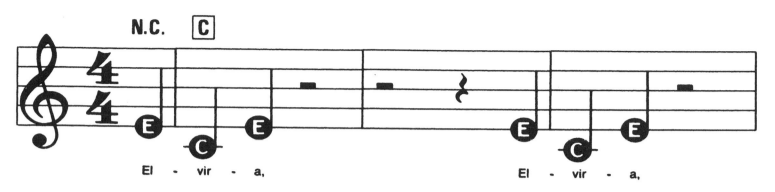

El - vir - a,   El - vir - a,

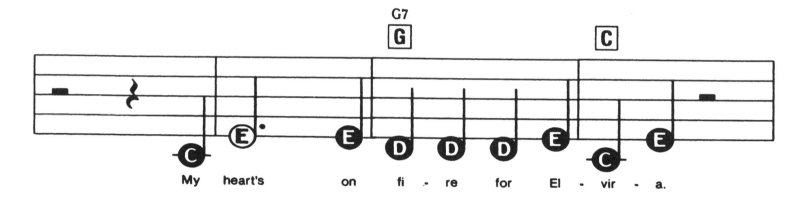

My heart's   on fi - re for El - vir - a.

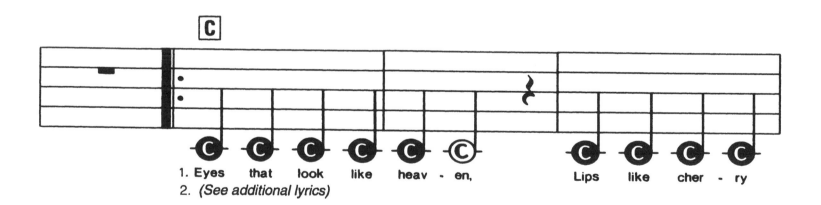

1. Eyes that look like heav - en,   Lips like cher - ry
2. (See additional lyrics)

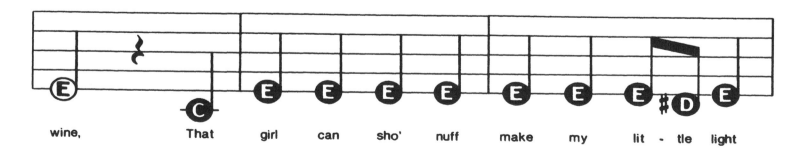

wine,   That girl can sho' nuff make my lit - tle light

shine. _____ I get a fun - ny

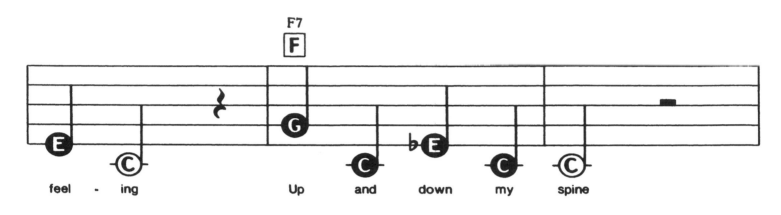

feel - ing Up and down my spine

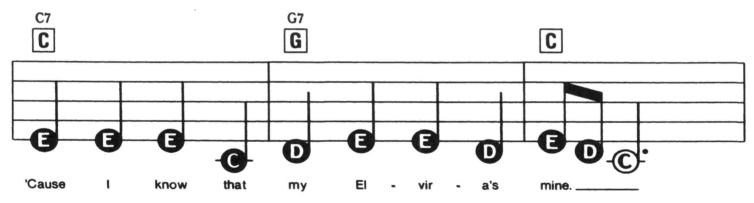

'Cause I know that my El - vir - a's mine. _____

CHORUS

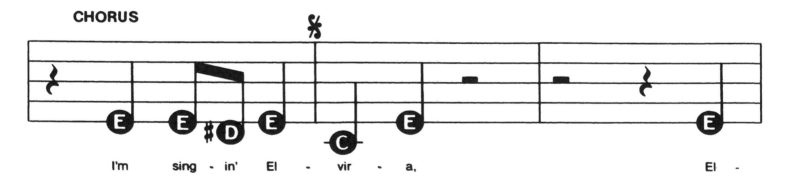

I'm sing - in' El - vir - a, El -

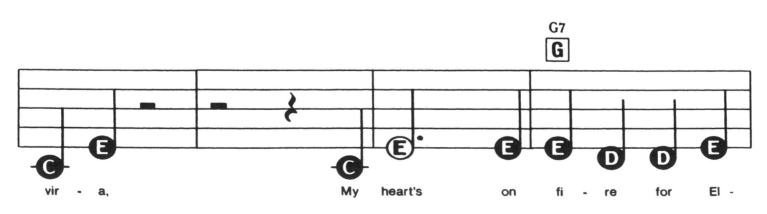

vir - a, My heart's on fi - re for El -

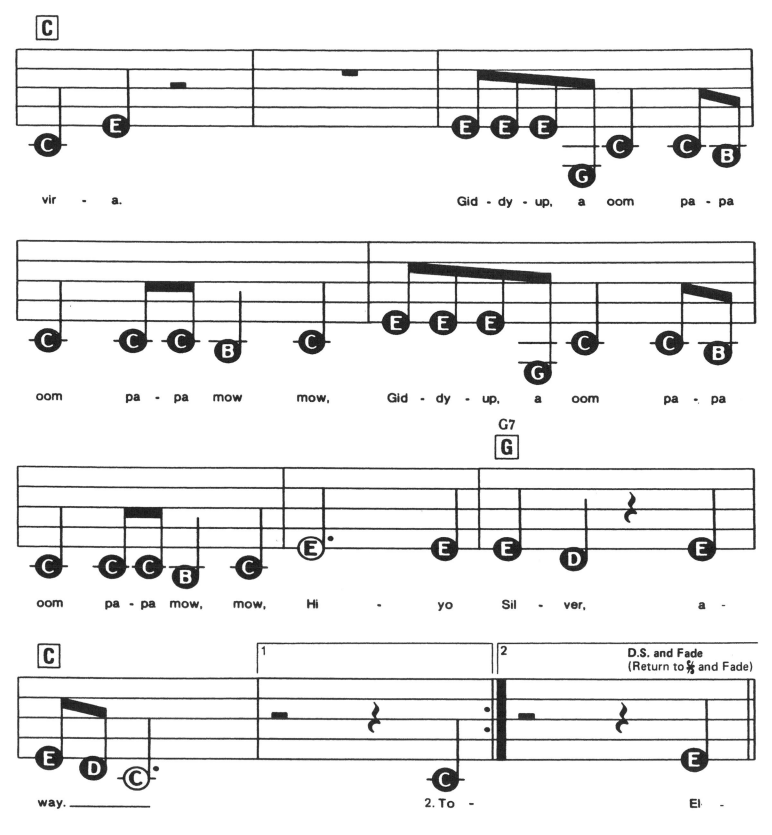

Additional Lyrics

2. Tonight I'm gonna meet her
   At the hungry house cafe
   And I'm gonna give her all the love I can
   She's gonna jump and holler
   'Cause I saved up my last two dollar
   And we're gonna search and find that preacher man.
   CHORUS

Here's a Quarter
(Call Someone Who Cares)

Registration 5
Rhythm: Waltz

Words and Music by
Travis Tritt

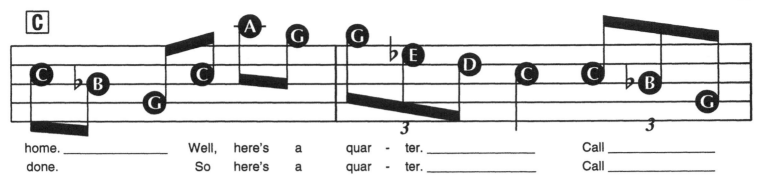

home. _____ Well, here's a quar - ter. _____ Call _____
done. _____ So here's a quar - ter. _____ Call _____

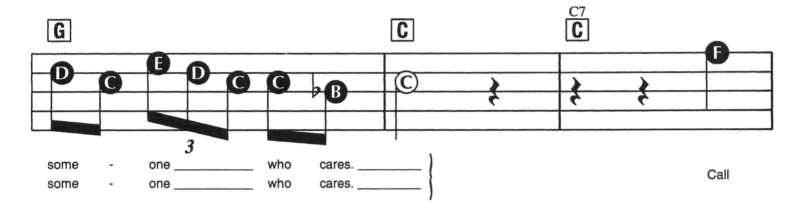

some - one _____ who cares. _____
some - one _____ who cares. _____
Call

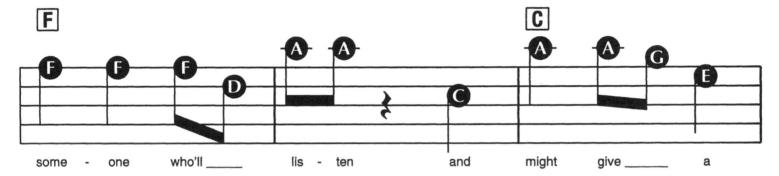

some - one who'll _____ lis - ten and might give _____ a

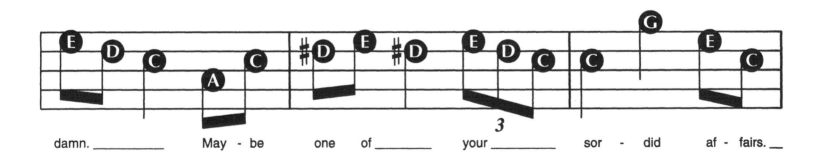

damn. _____ May - be one of _____ your _____ sor - did af - fairs. __

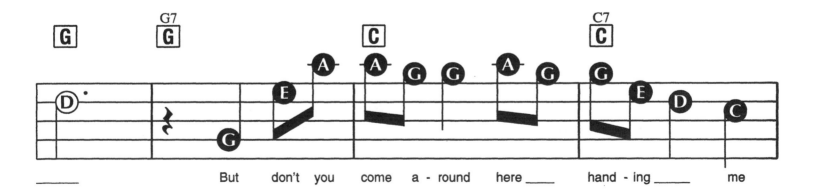

_____ But don't you come a - round here ____ hand - ing _____ me

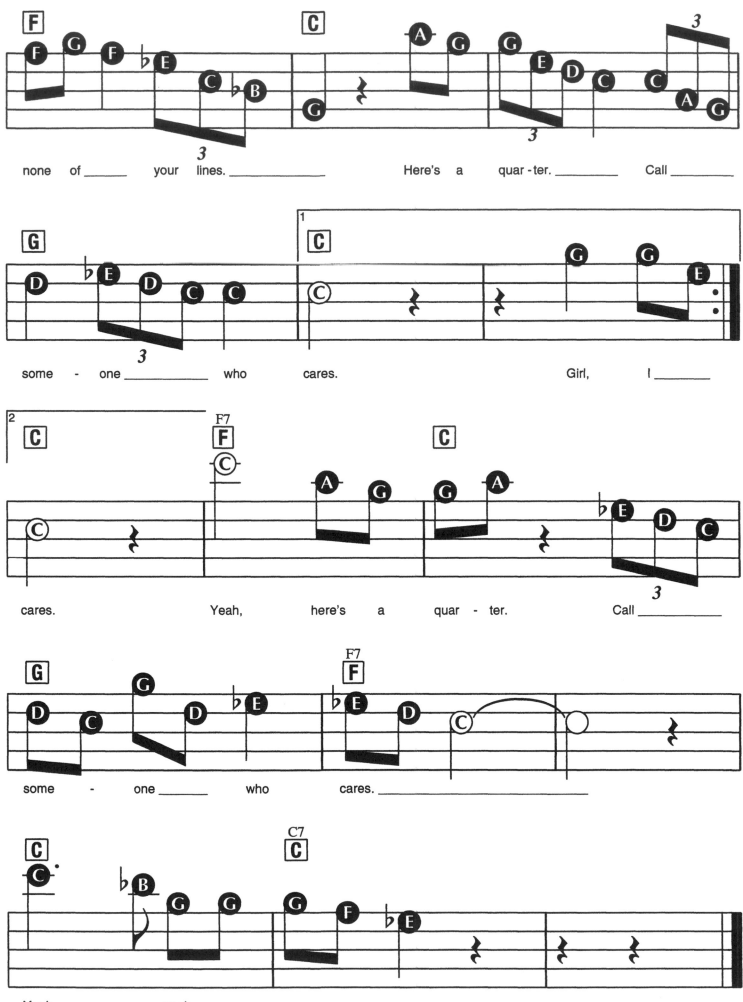

Jealous Heart

Registration 7
Rhythm: Country or Fox Trot

Words and Music by
Jenny Lou Carson

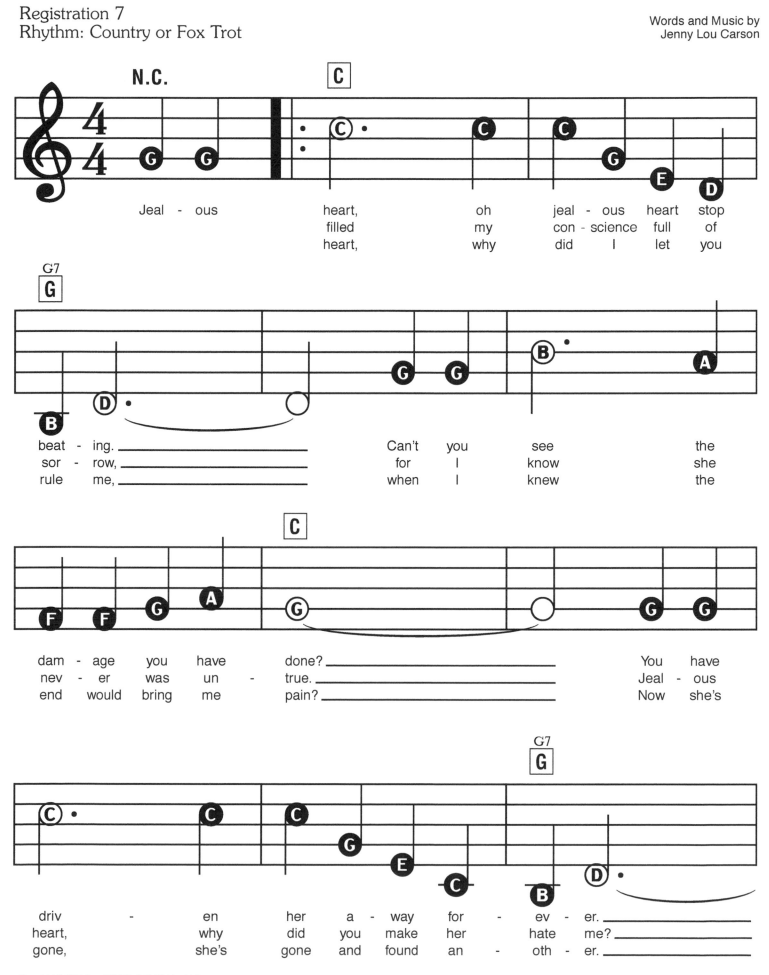

68

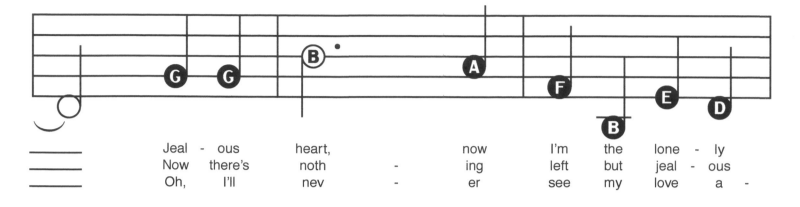

Jeal - ous heart, now I'm the lone - ly
Now there's noth - ing left but jeal - ous
Oh, I'll nev - er see my love a -

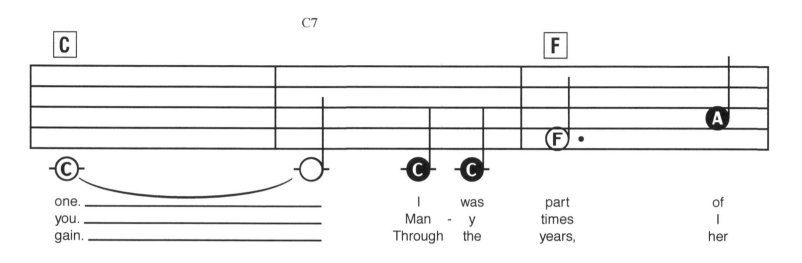

C7   F

one. I was part of
you. Man - y times I
gain. Through the years, her

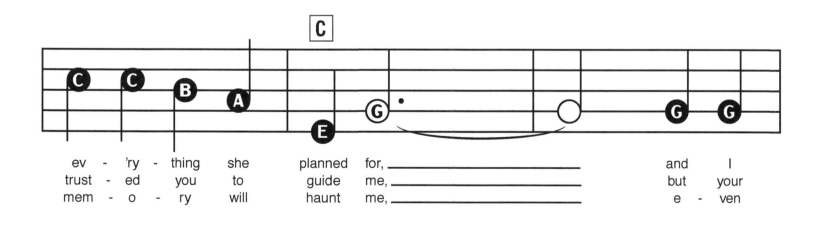

C

ev - 'ry - thing she planned for, and I
trust - ed you to guide me, but your
mem - o - ry will haunt me, e - ven

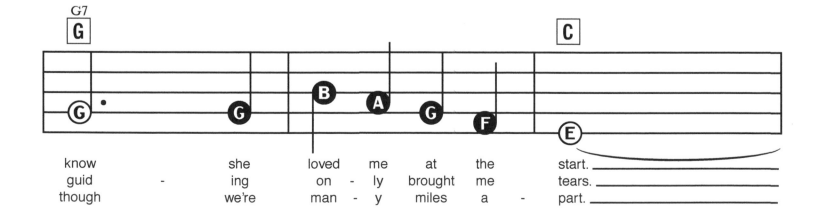

G7
G   C

know she loved me at the start.
guid - ing on - ly brought me tears.
though we're man - y miles a - part.

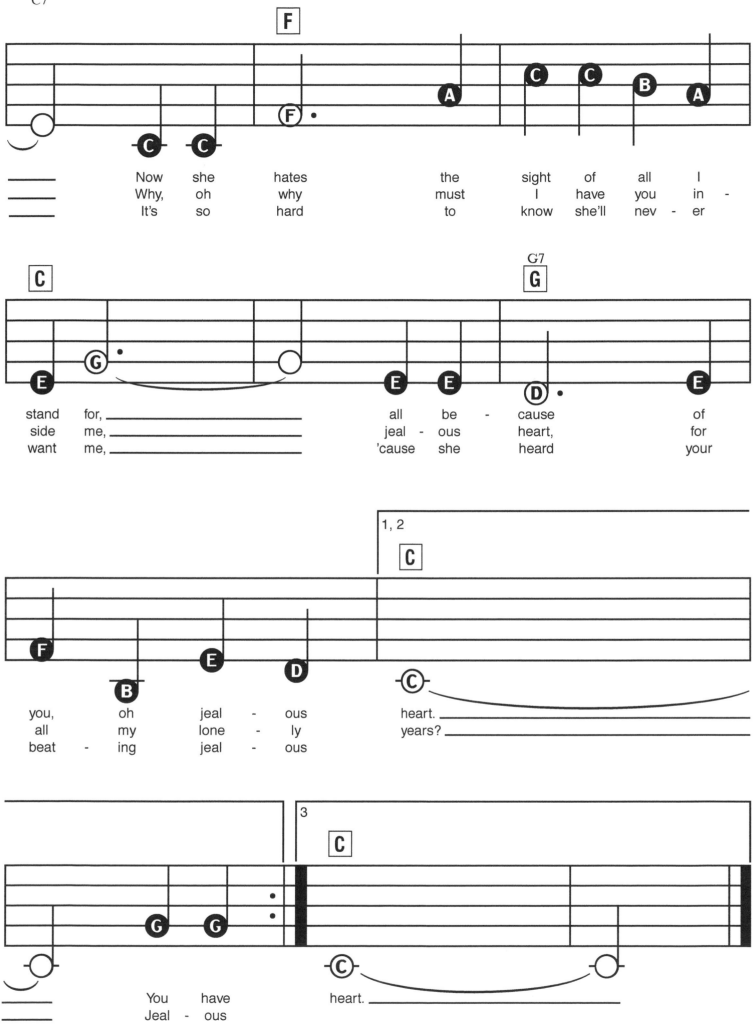

Honky Tonk Blues

Registration 5
Rhythm: Rock or Swing

Words and Music by
Hank Williams

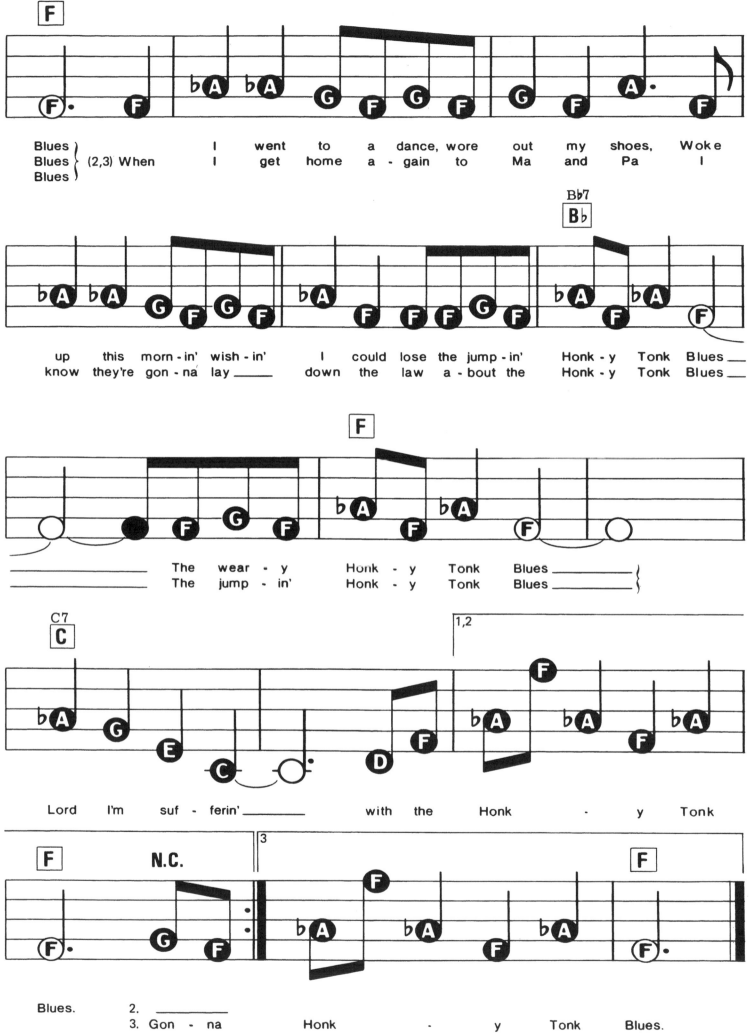

Blues }
Blues } (2,3) When I went to a dance, wore out my shoes, Woke
Blues }

(2,3) When I get home a-gain to Ma and Pa I

up this morn-in' wish-in' I could lose the jump-in' Honk-y Tonk Blues ___
know they're gon-na lay ___ down the law a-bout the Honk-y Tonk Blues ___

___ The wear-y Honk-y Tonk Blues ___ }
___ The jump-in' Honk-y Tonk Blues ___ }

Lord I'm suf-ferin' ___ with the Honk - y Tonk

Blues. 2. ___
3. Gon-na Honk - y Tonk Blues.

I Can't Help It
(If I'm Still in Love with You)

Registration 3
Rhythm: Fox Trot or Ballad

Words and Music by
Hank Williams

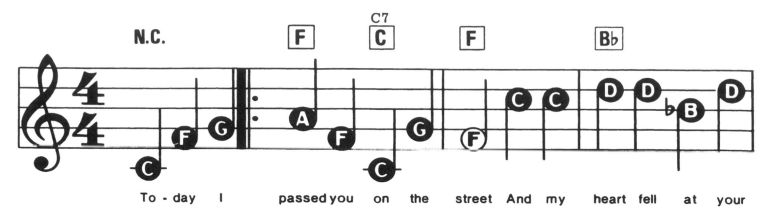

To - day I passed you on the street And my heart fell at your

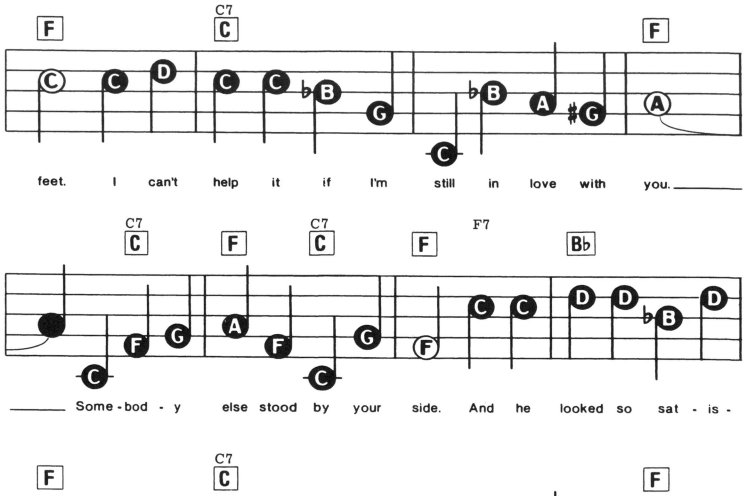

feet. I can't help it if I'm still in love with you. _____

_____ Some - bod - y else stood by your side. And he looked so sat - is -

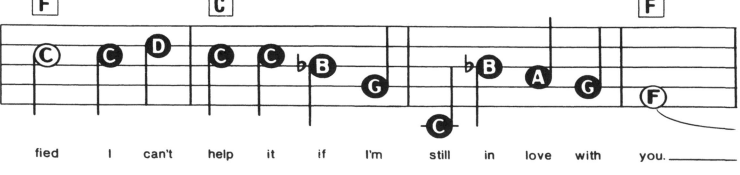

fied I can't help it if I'm still in love with you. _____

73

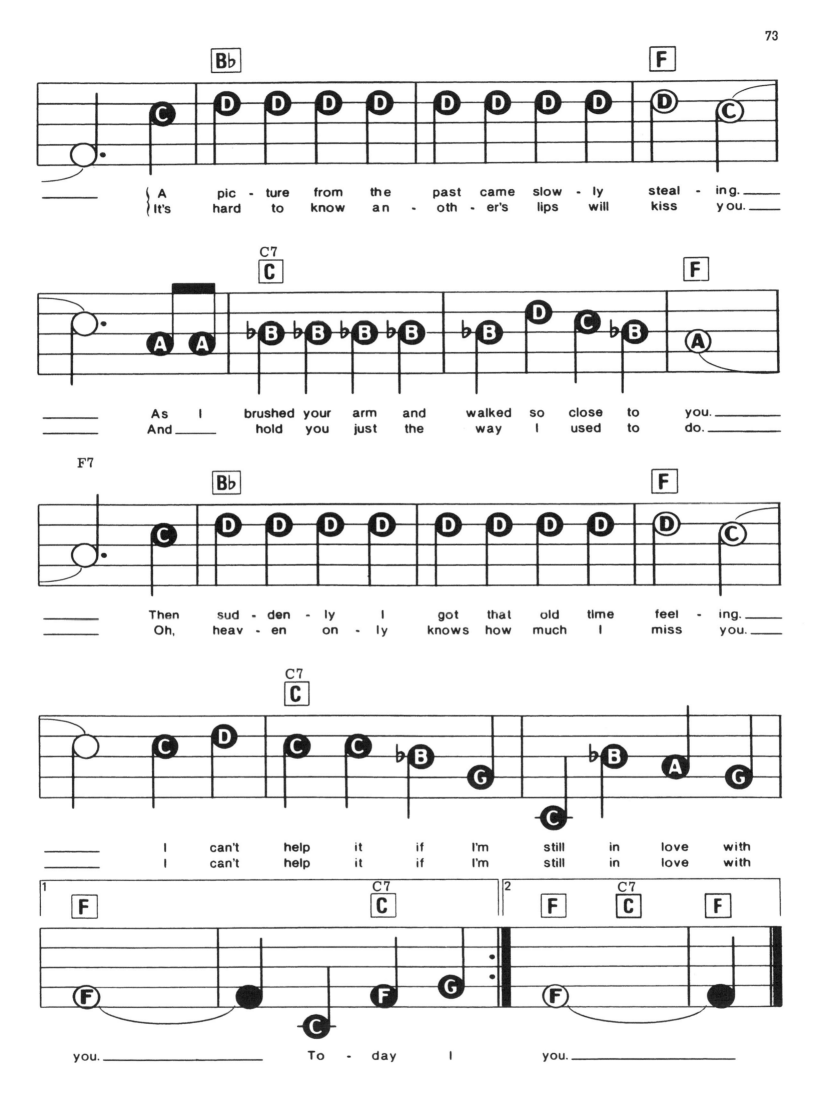

(I Never Promised You A)
Rose Garden

Registration 4
Rhythm: Fox Trot

Words and Music by
Joe South

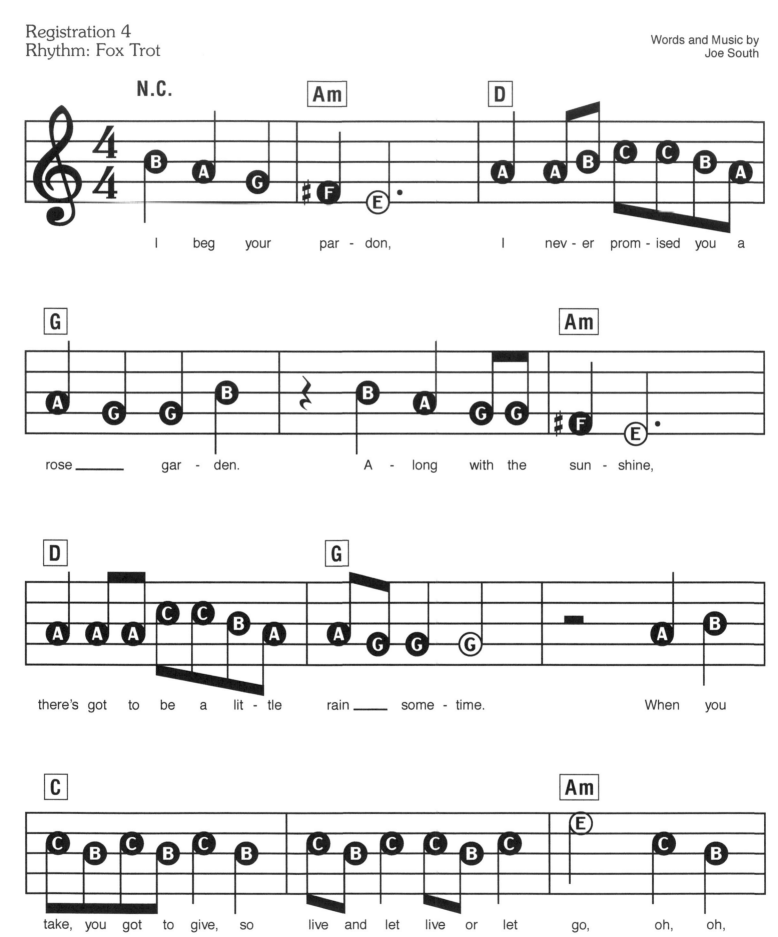

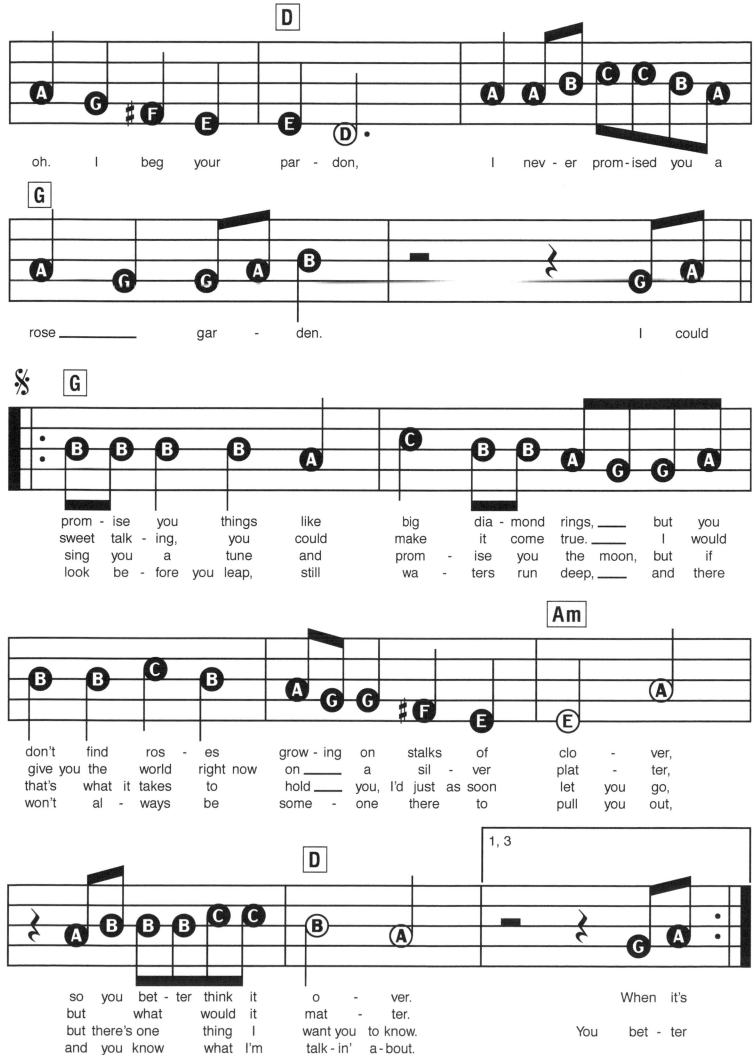

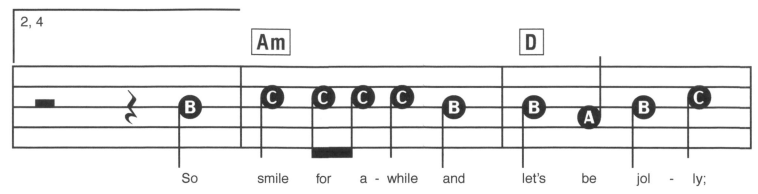

So smile for a - while and let's be jol - ly;

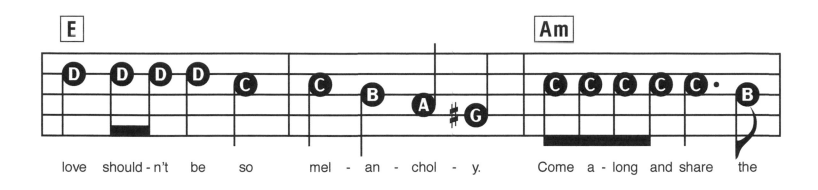

love should - n't be so mel - an - chol - y. Come a - long and share the

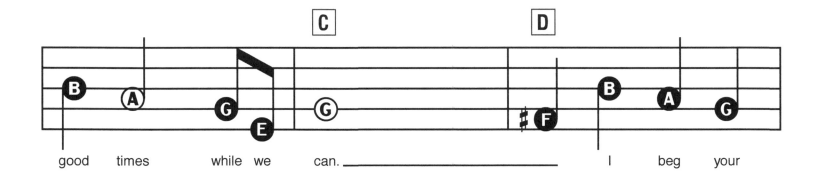

good times while we can. _____ I beg your

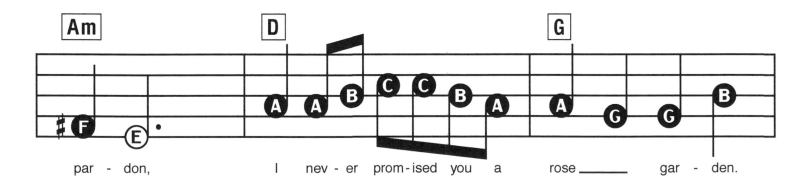

par - don, I nev - er prom - ised you a rose _____ gar - den.

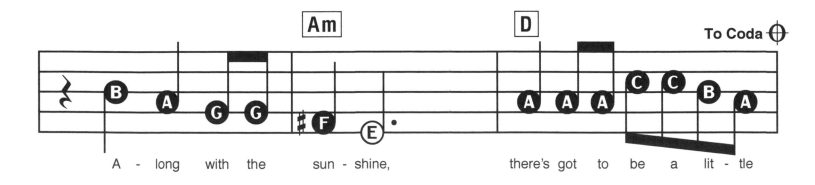

A - long with the sun - shine, there's got to be a lit - tle

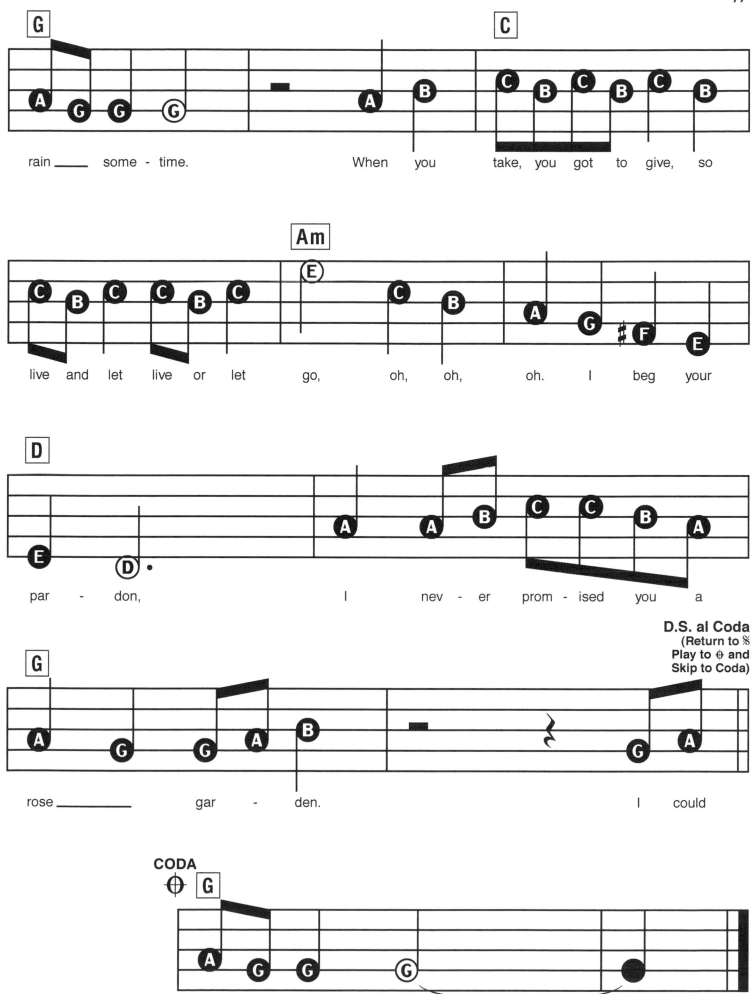

I Wouldn't Have Missed It for the World

Registration 5
Rhythm: Rock

Words and Music by Kye Fleming,
Dennis Morgan and Charles Quillen

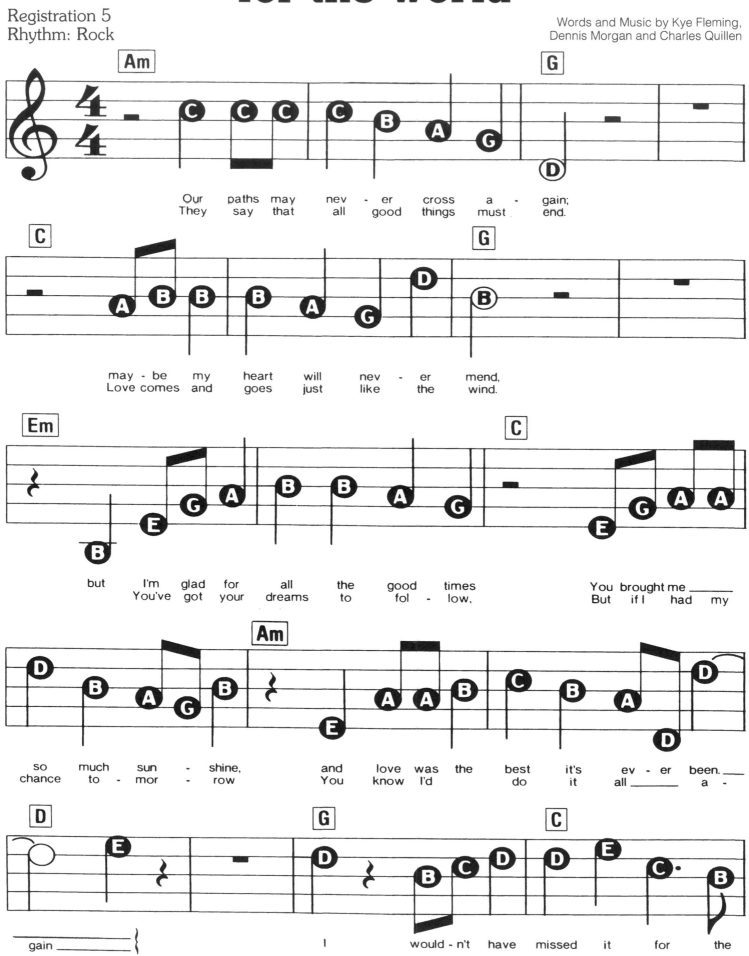

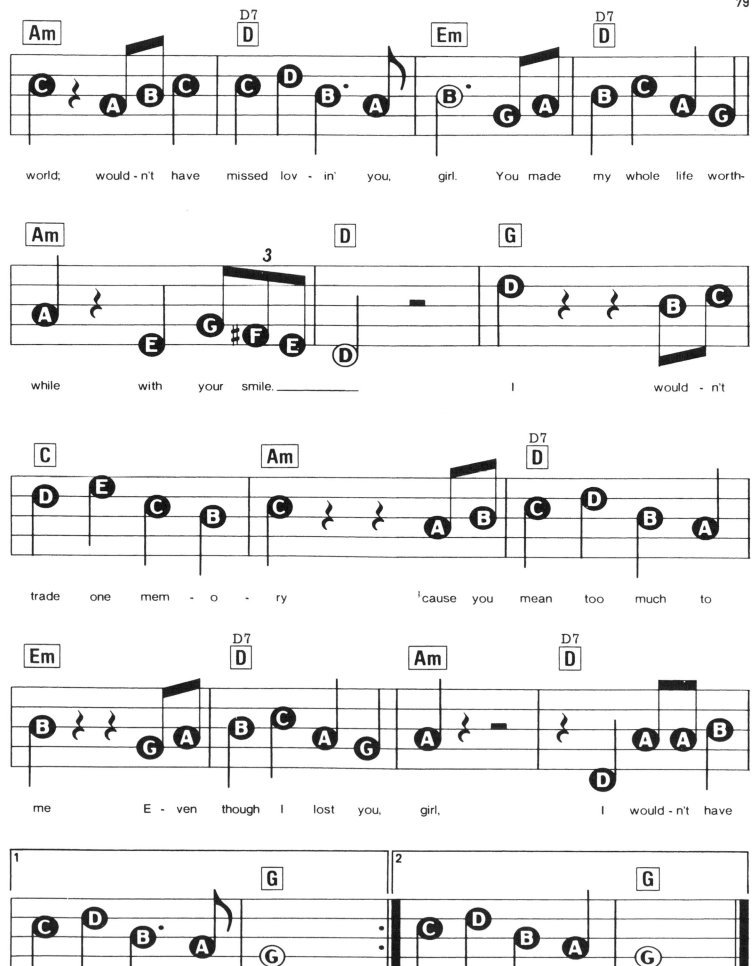

world; would-n't have missed lov-in' you, girl. You made my whole life worth-

while with your smile._____ I would-n't

trade one mem - o - ry 'cause you mean too much to

me E - ven though I lost you, girl, I would-n't have

missed it for the world.   missed it for the world.

I.O.U.

Registration 10
Rhythm: Ballad

Words and Music by Kerry Chater
and Austin Roberts

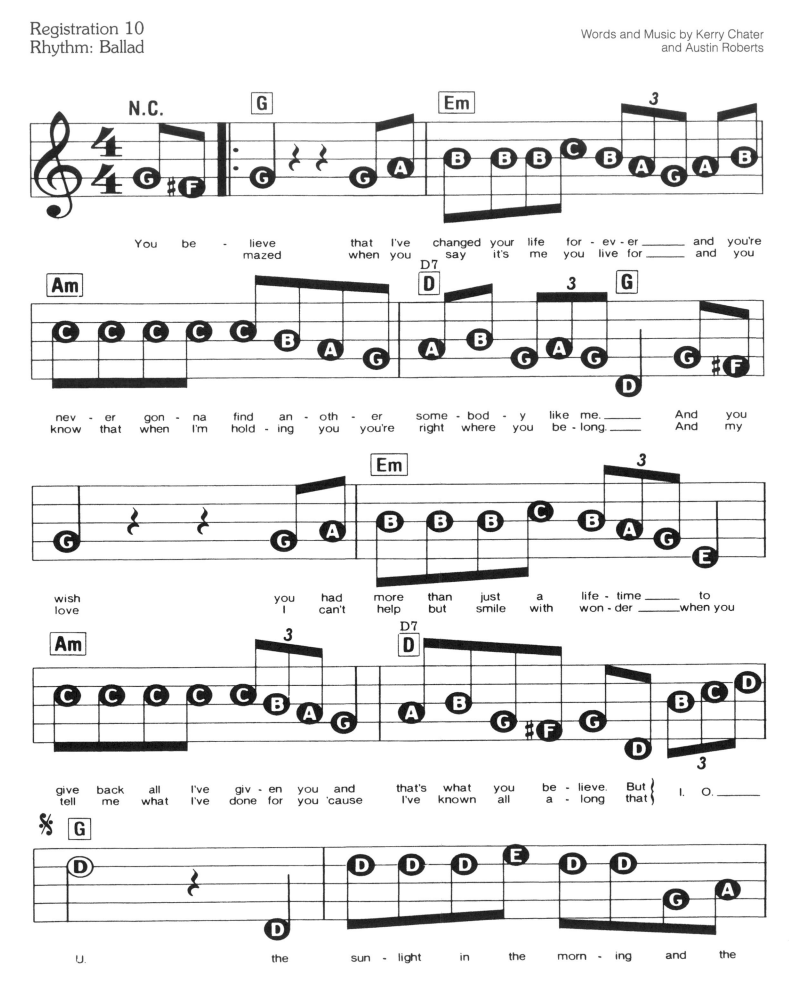

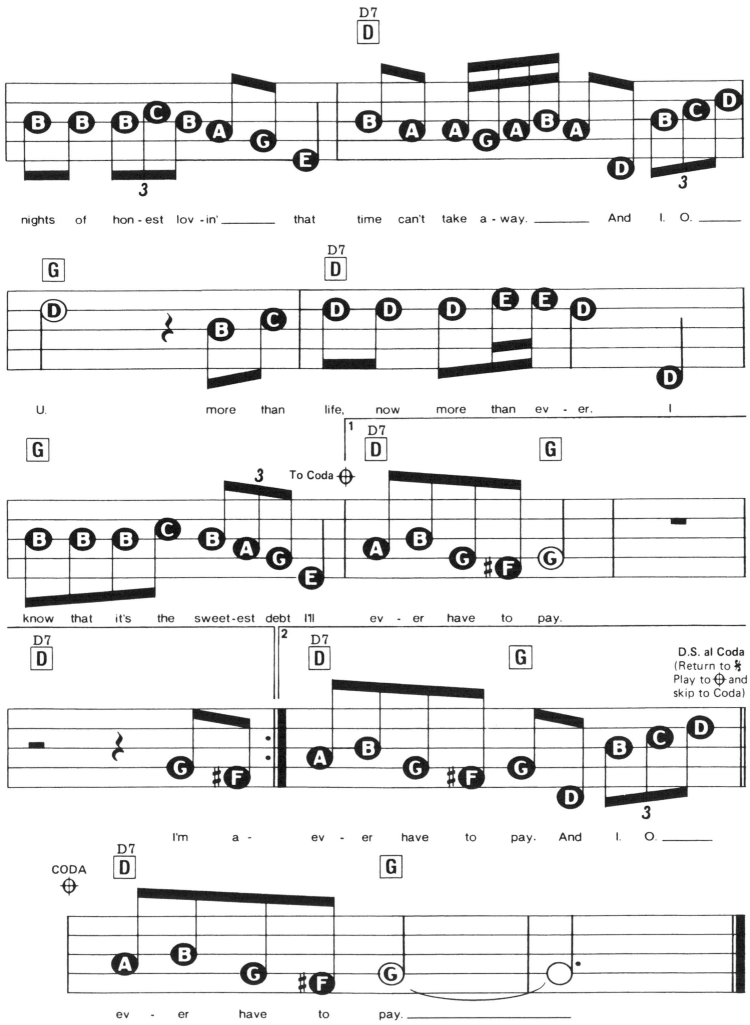

Last Date

Registration 8
Rhythm: Slow Rock or Country Swing

By Floyd Cramer

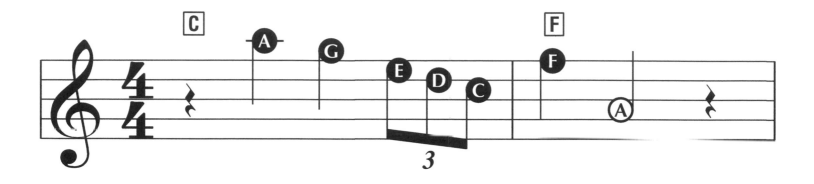

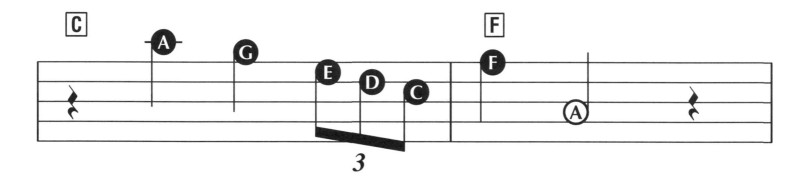

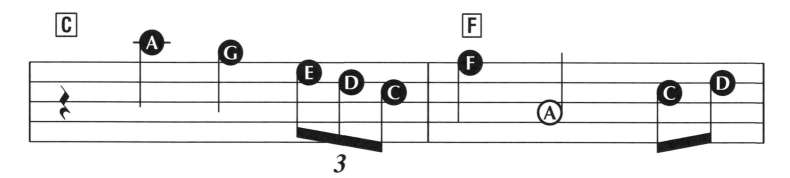

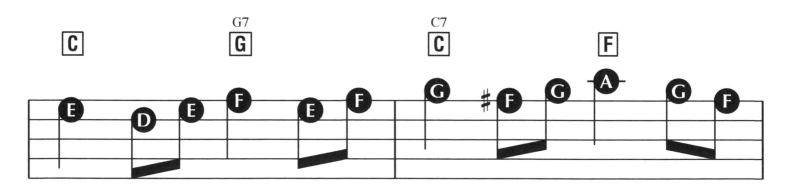

83

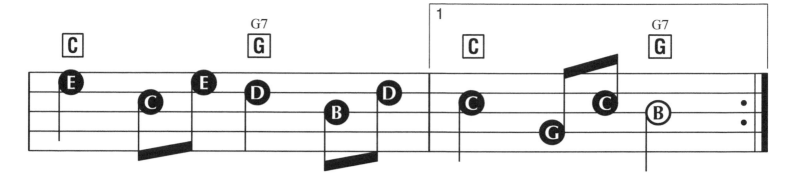

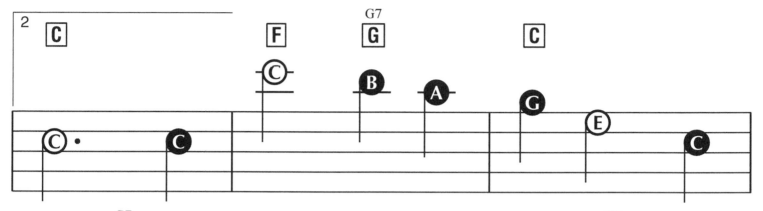

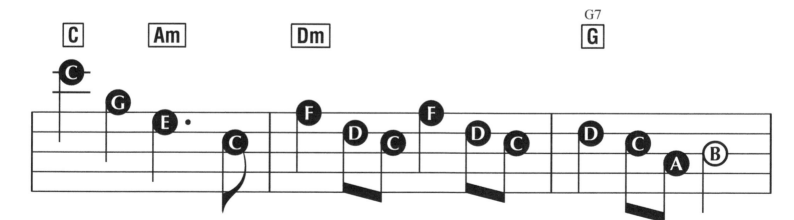

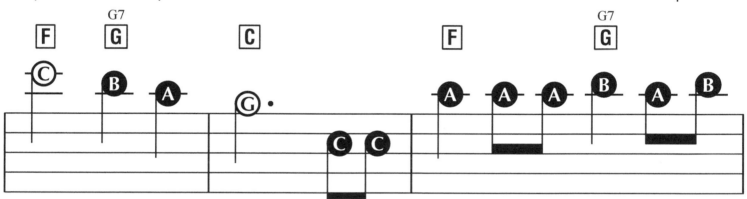

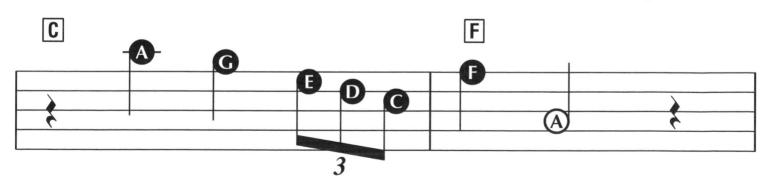

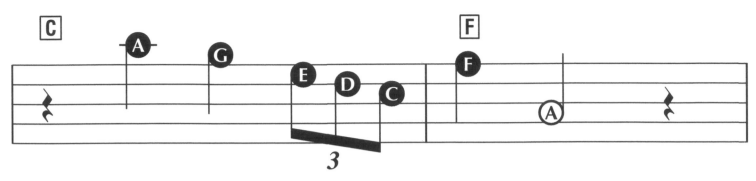

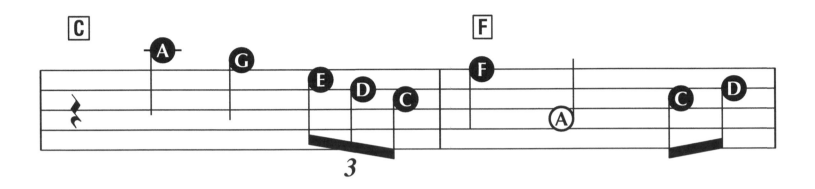

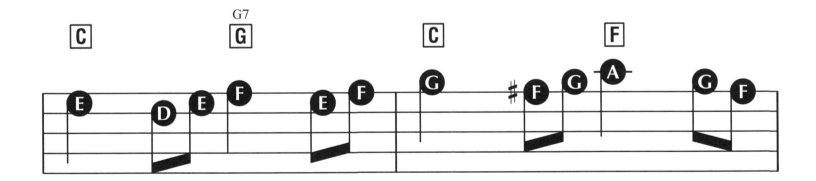

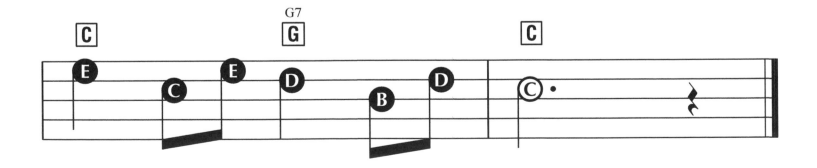

Kaw-Liga

Registration 4
Rhythm: Fox Trot or Ballad

Words and Music by Hank Williams
and Fred Rose

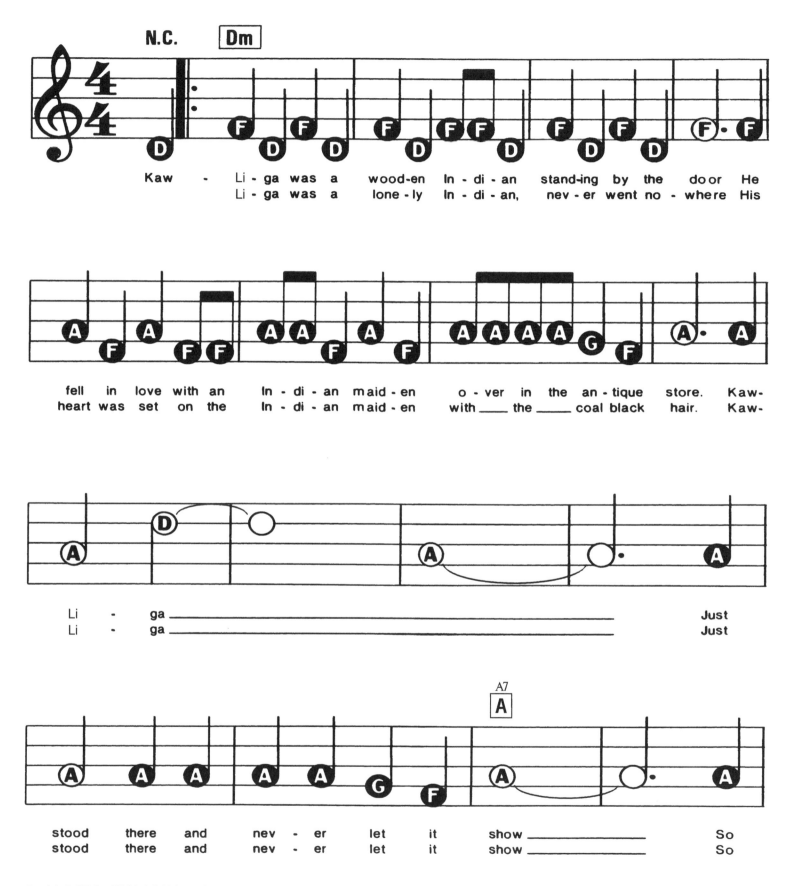

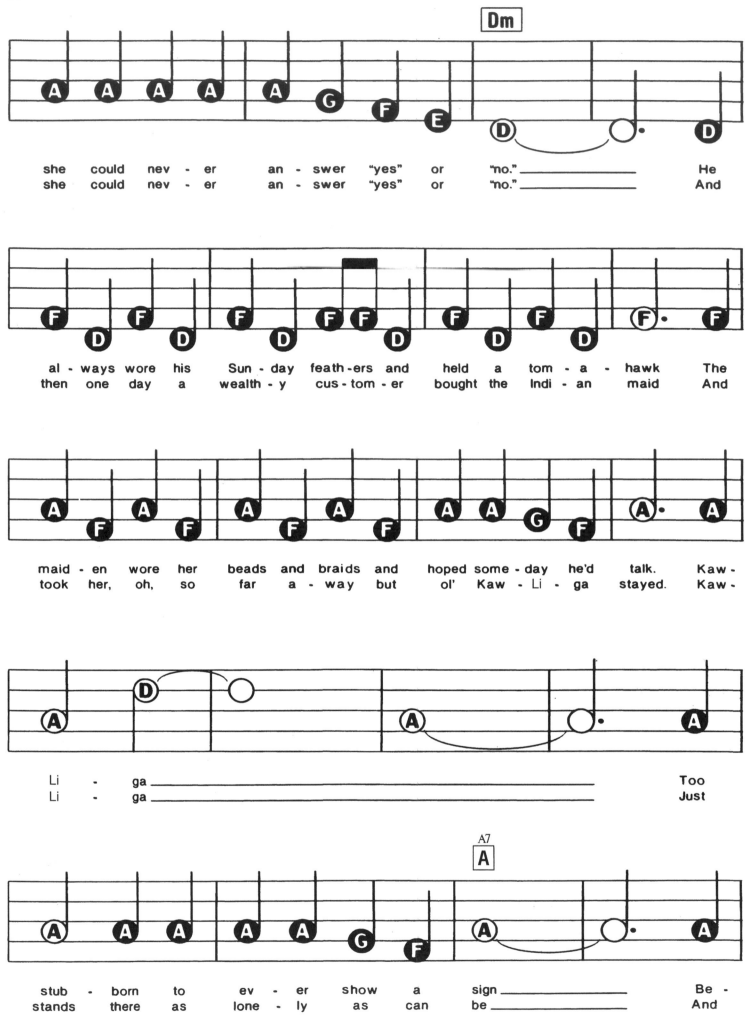

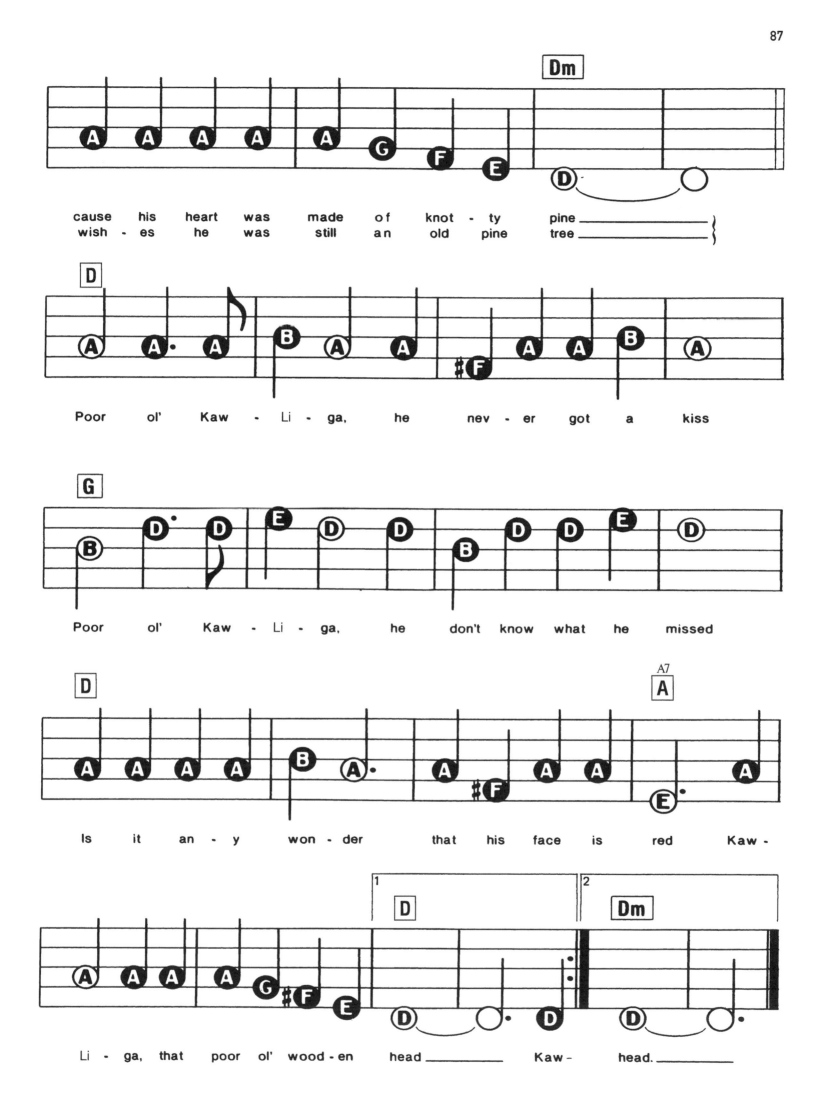

Little Green Apples

Registration 3
Rhythm: Country

Words and Music by
Bobby Russell

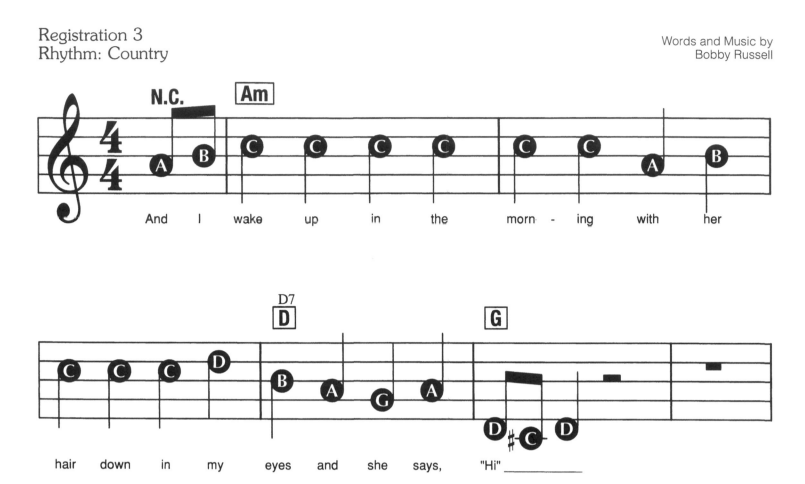

And I wake up in the morn - ing with her

hair down in my eyes and she says, "Hi" _____

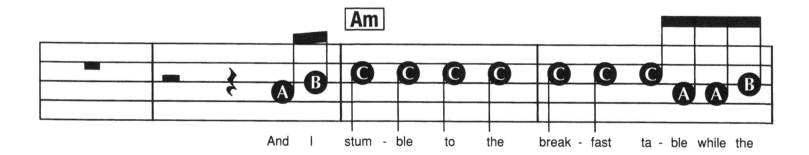

And I stum - ble to the break - fast ta - ble while the

kids are go - ing off to school, good - bye. _____

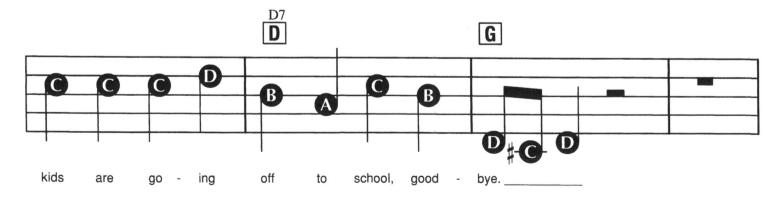

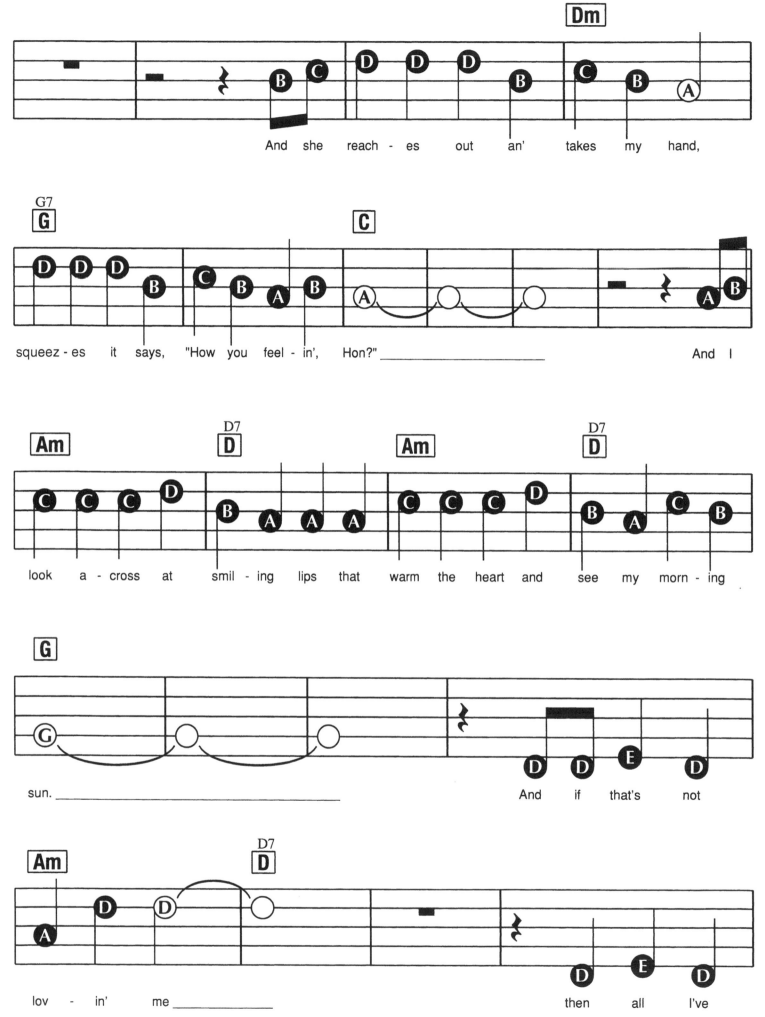

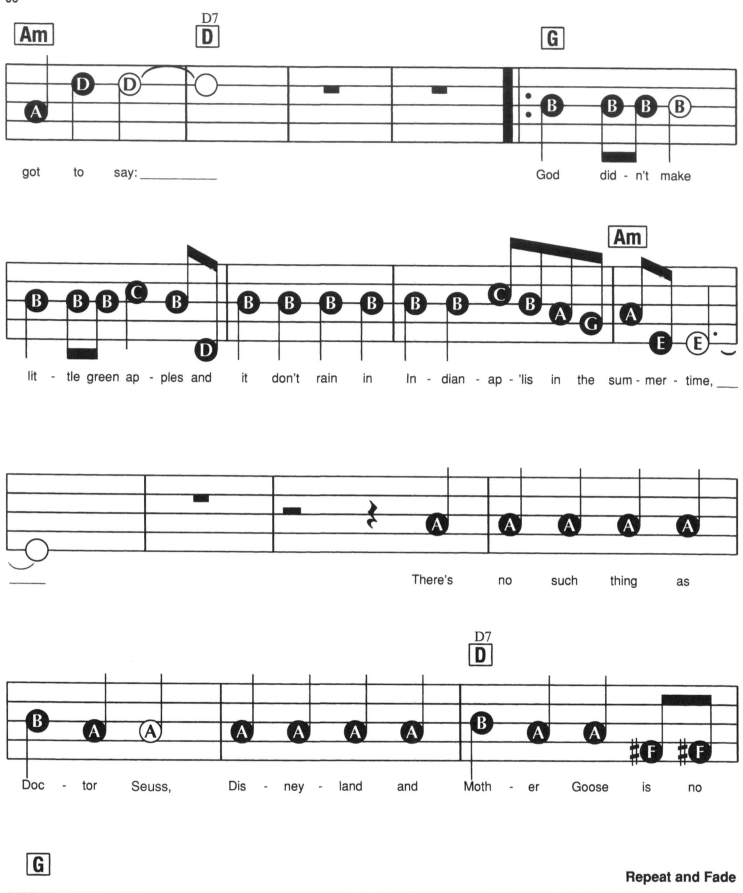

got to say: _____

God did - n't make

lit - tle green ap - ples and it don't rain in In - dian - ap - 'lis in the sum - mer - time, ___

___ There's no such thing as

Doc - tor Seuss, Dis - ney - land and Moth - er Goose is no

Repeat and Fade

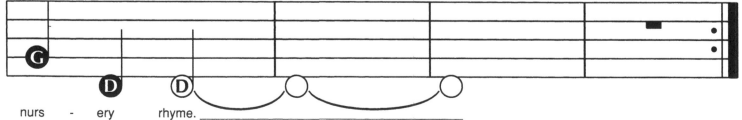

nurs - ery rhyme. ___

Singing the Blues

Registration 9
Rhythm: Shuffle

Words and Music by
Melvin Endsley

Well, I nev - er felt more like sing - ing the blues 'cause

I nev - er thought that I'd ev - er lose your love, dear,

Why'd you do me this way? _____ Well, I

nev - er felt more like cry - ing all night 'cause ev - 'ry - thing's wrong and

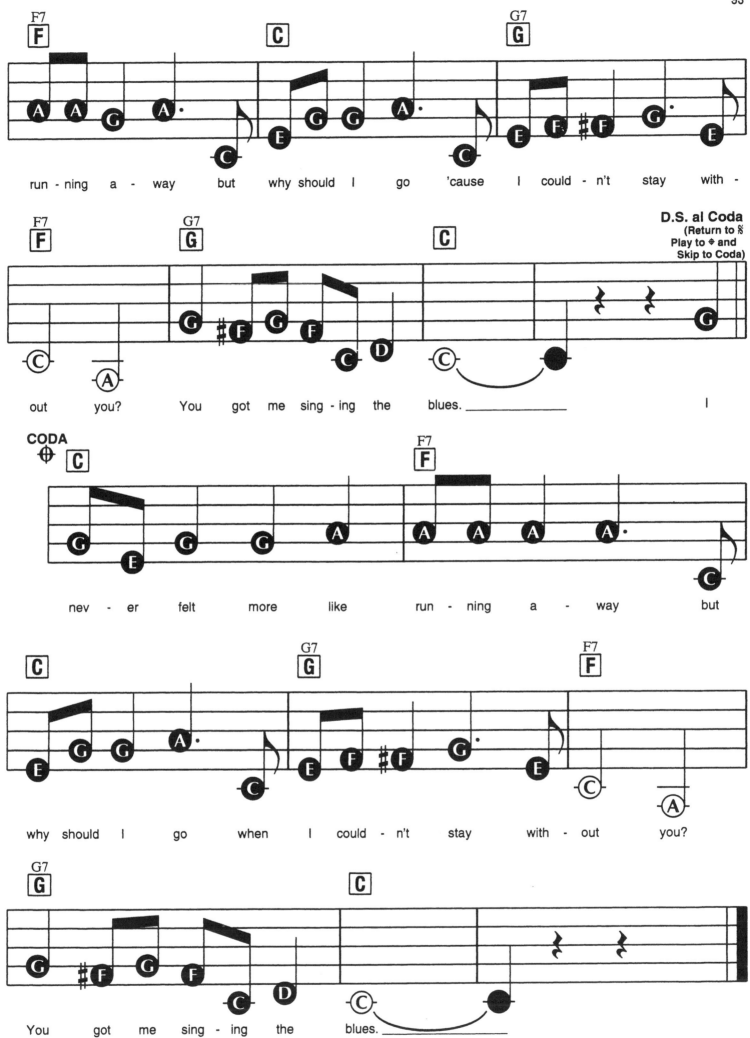

D.S. al Coda
(Return to 𝄋
Play to ⊕ and
Skip to Coda)

Lookin' for Love
from URBAN COWBOY

Registration 7
Rhythm: Country or Rock

Words and Music by Wanda Mallette,
Patti Ryan and Bob Morrison

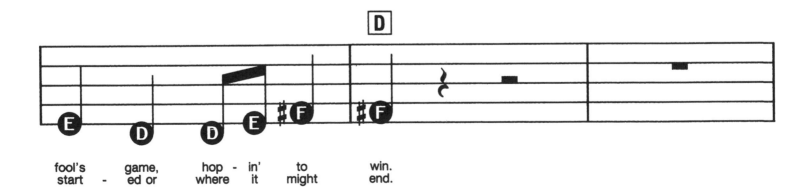

Well, I've spent a life - time look - in' for you.
And I was a - lone then; no love in sight.

Sin - gles bars and good - time lov - ers were
I did ev - 'ry - thing I could to get me

nev - er true.
through the night.

Don't Play - in' a
know where it

fool's game, hop - in' to win.
start - ed or where it might end.

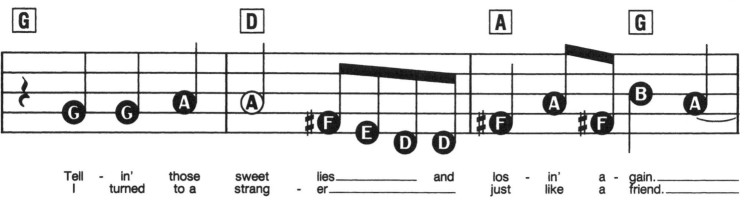

Tell - in' those sweet lies_____ and los - in' a - gain._____
I turned to a strang - er_____ just like a friend._____

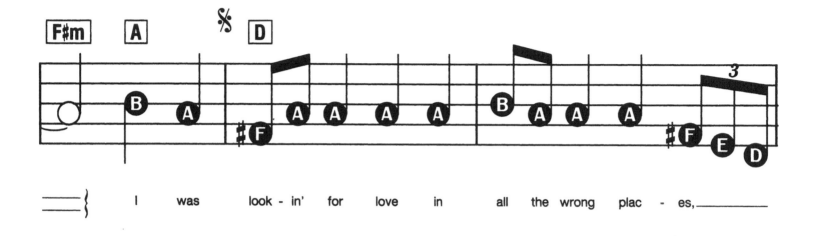

I was look - in' for love in all the wrong plac - es,_____

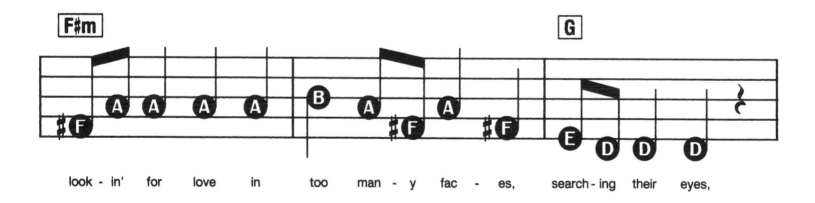

look - in' for love in too man - y fac - es, search - ing their eyes,

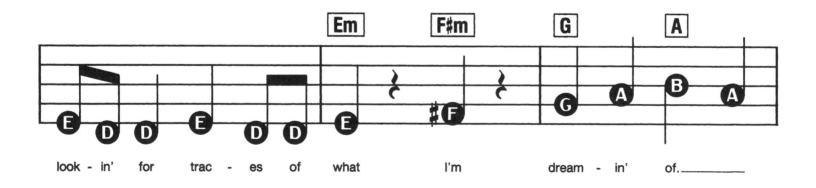

look - in' for trac - es of what I'm dream - in' of._____

96

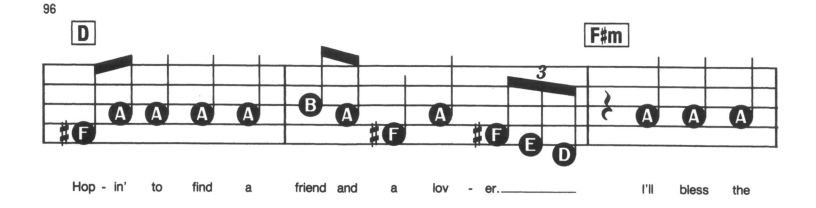

Hop - in' to find a friend and a lov - er._____ I'll bless the

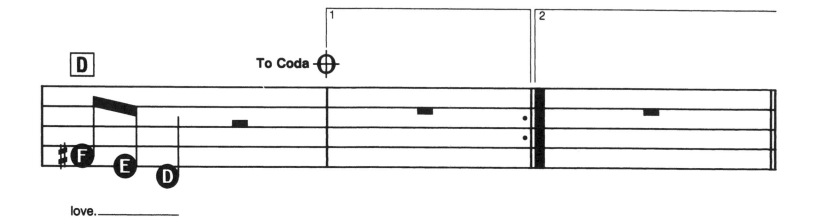

day I dis - cov - er an - oth - er heart looking' for

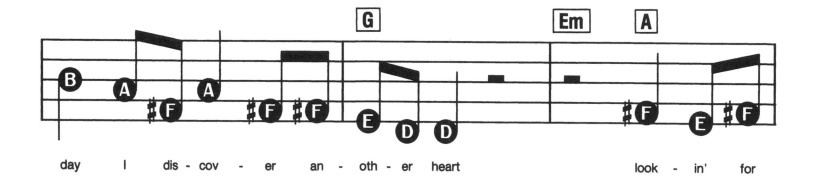

love._____

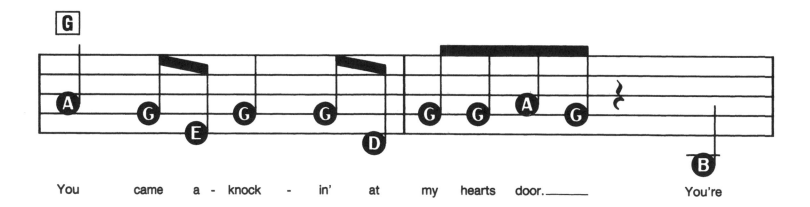

You came a - knock - in' at my hearts door._____ You're

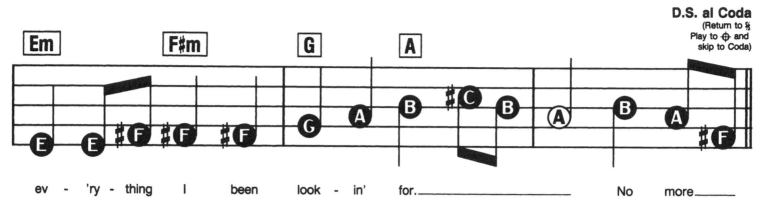

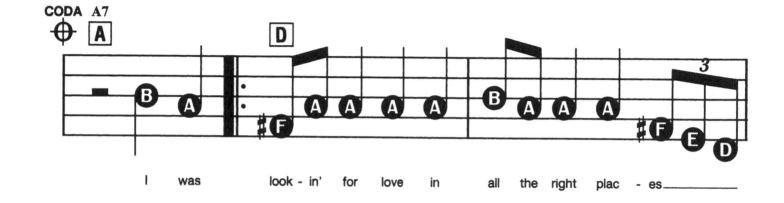

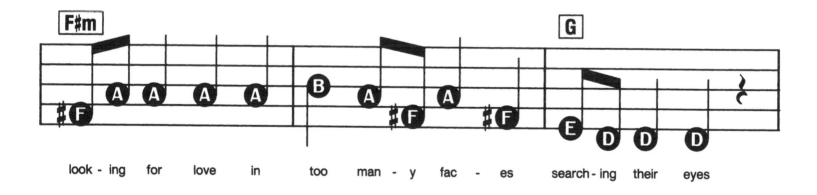

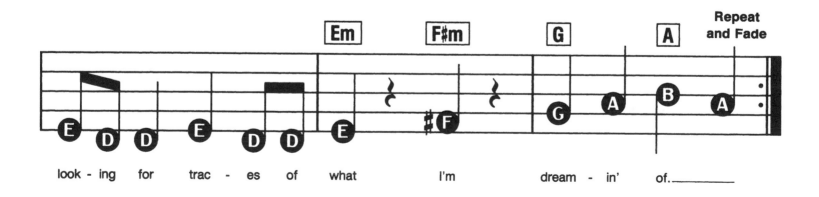

On the Road Again

Registration 7
Rhythm: Swing

Words and Music by
Willie Nelson

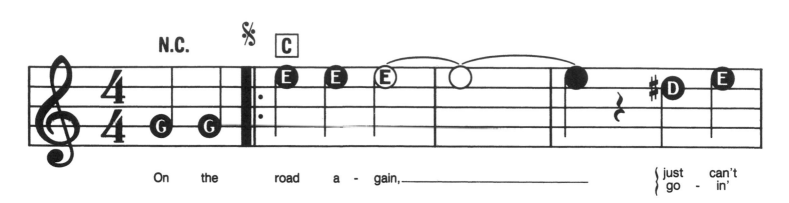

On the road a - gain,_____ { just can't / go - in'

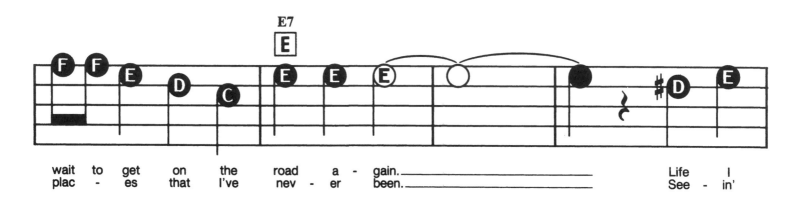

wait to get on the road a - gain._____ Life I
plac - es that I've nev - er been._____ See - in'

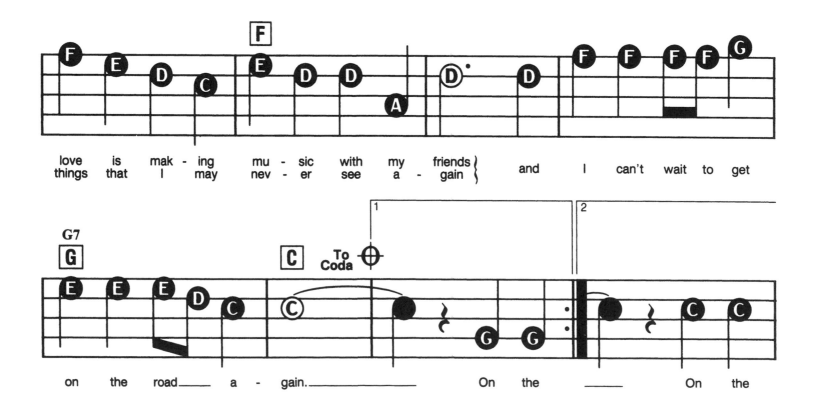

love is mak - ing mu - sic with my friends { and I can't wait to get
things that I may nev - er see a - gain {

on the road_____ a - gain._____ On the _____ On the

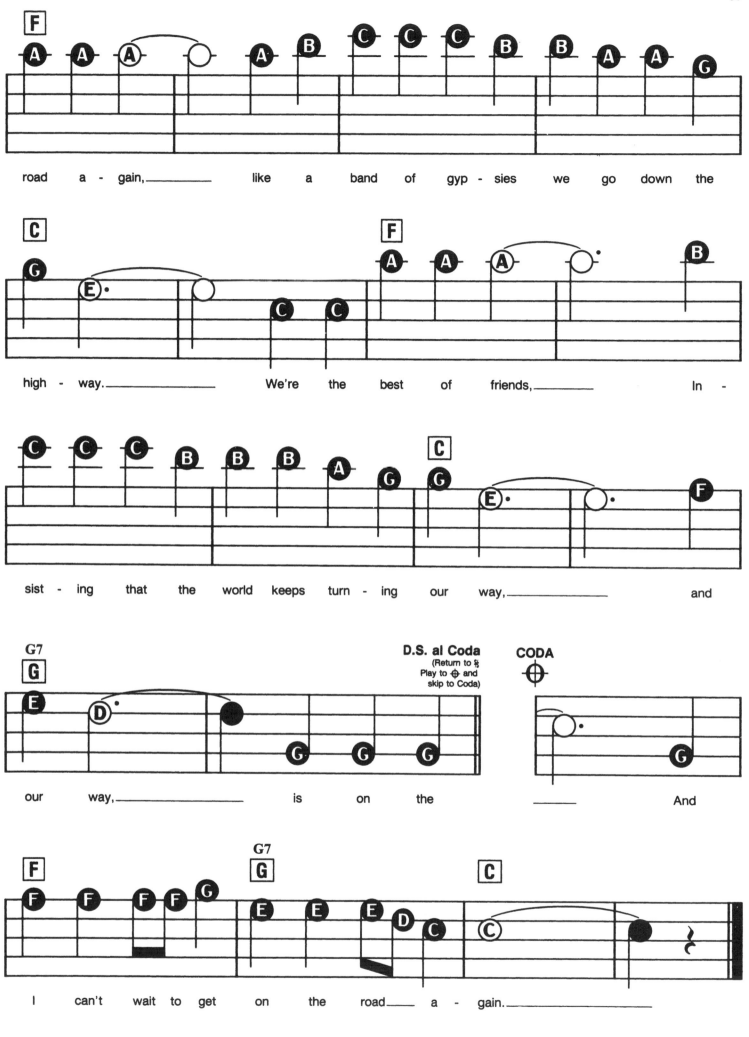

One Has My Name, the Other Has My Heart

Registration 4
Rhythm: Country Swing

Words and Music by Eddie Dean,
Dearest Dean and Hal Blair

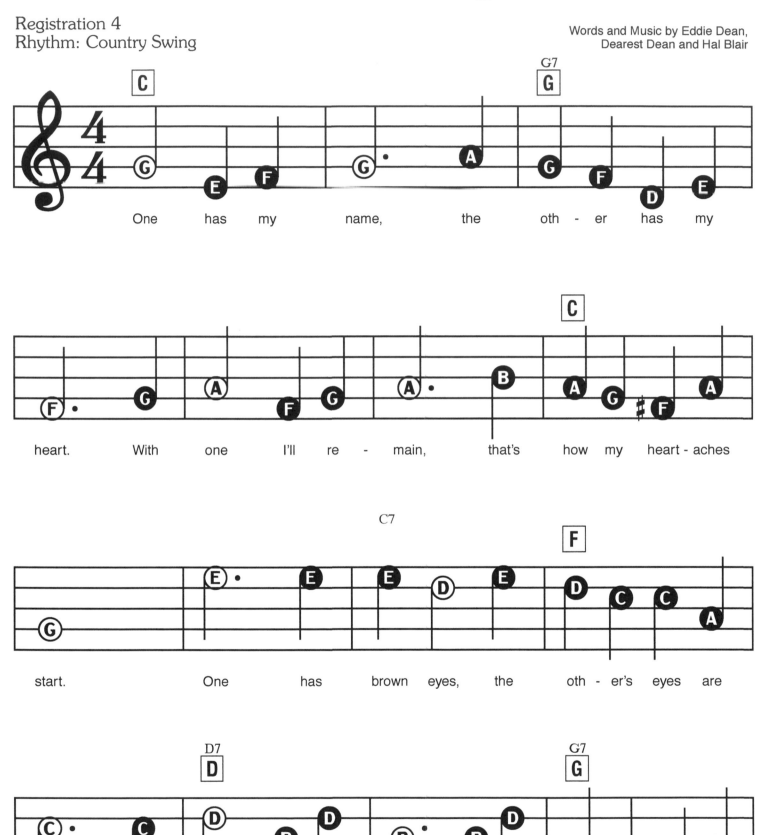

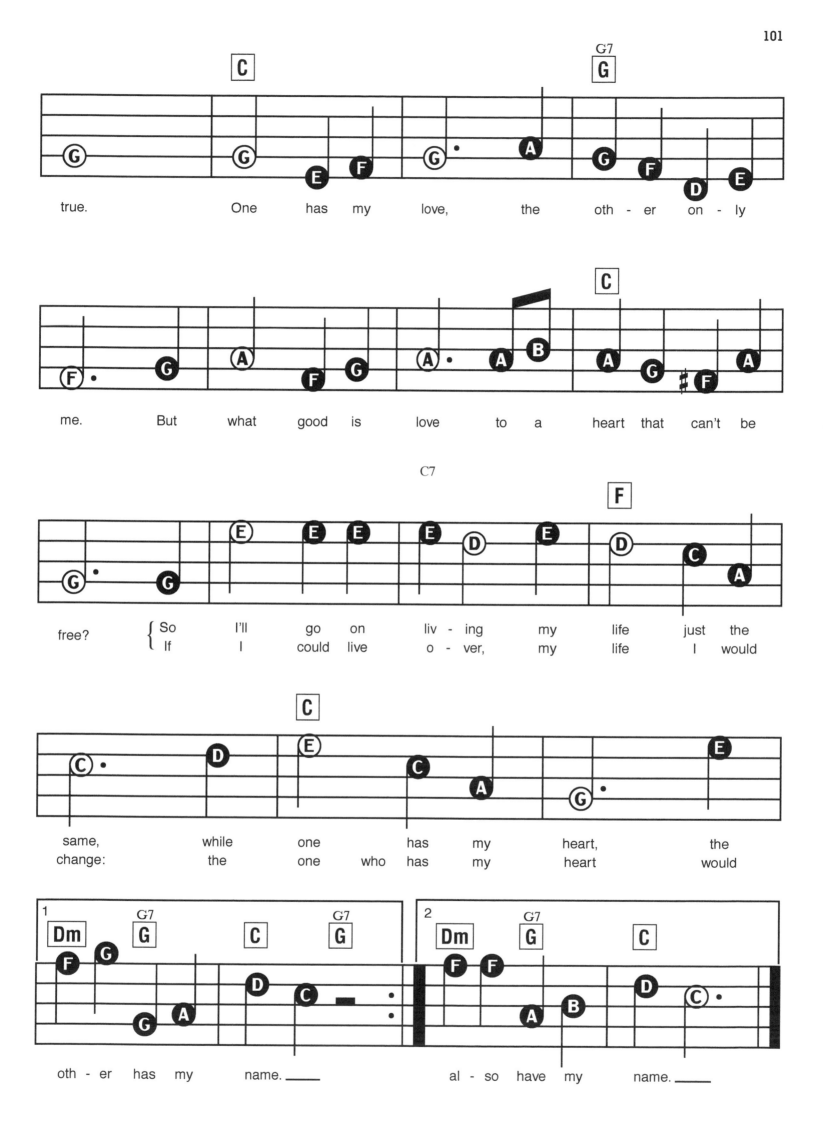

Please Help Me, I'm Falling
(In Love with You)

Registration 10
Rhythm: Ballad or Country Western

Words and Music by Don Robertson
and Hal Blair

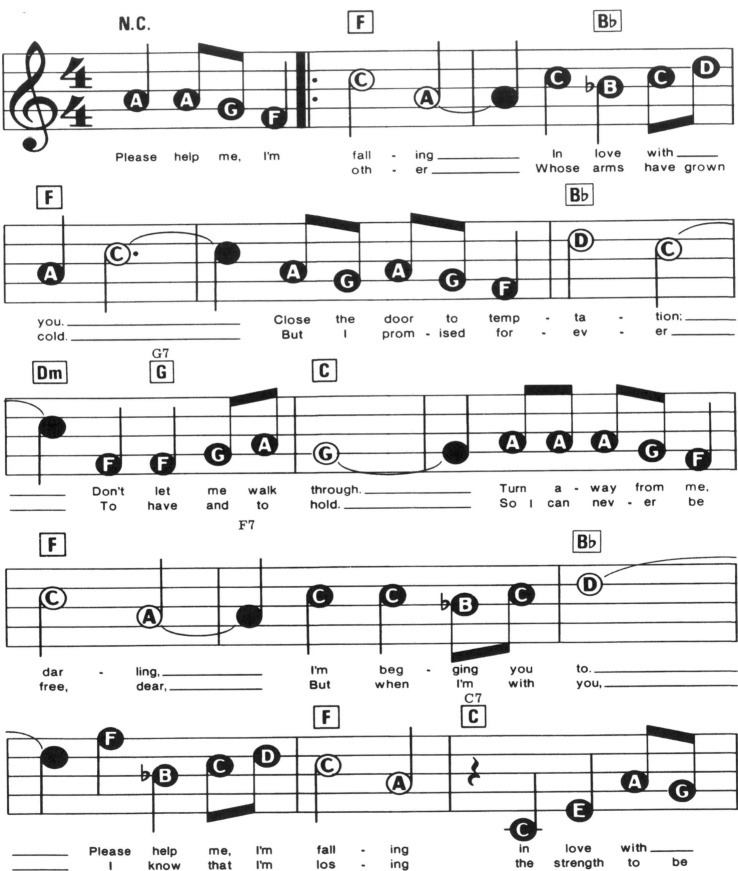

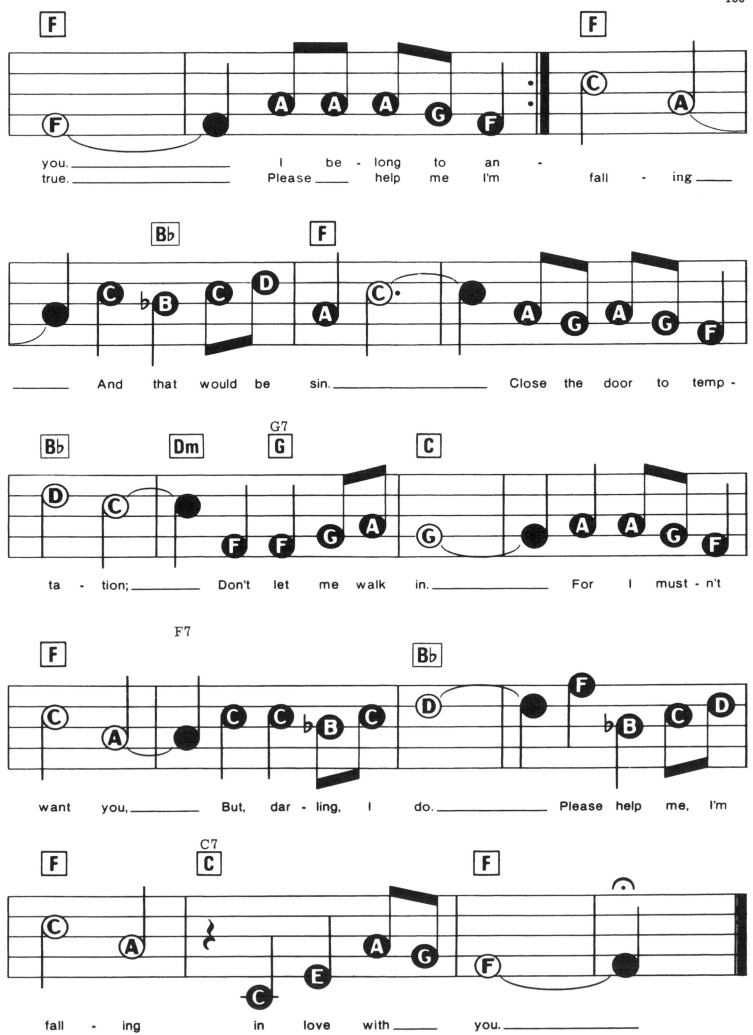

Rednecks, White Socks and Blue Ribbon Beer

Registration 4
Rhythm: Rock or 8-Beat

Words and Music by Chuck Neese,
Bob McDill and Wayland Holyfield

The bar - maid is mad _____ 'cause some ___ guy _____ made a

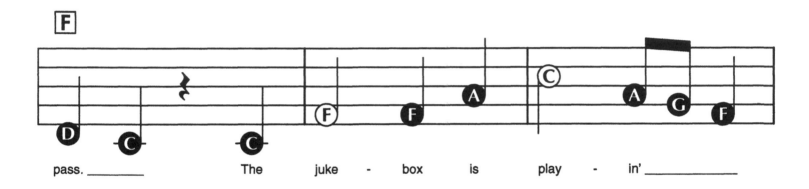

pass. _____ The juke - box is play - in' _____

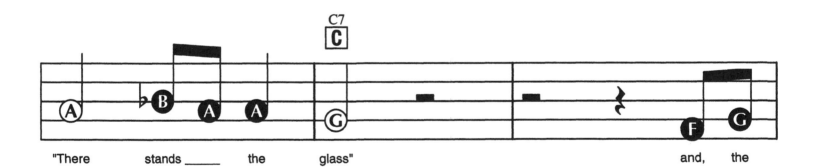

"There stands _____ the glass" and, the

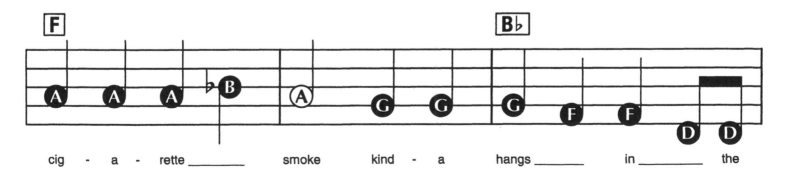

cig - a - rette _____ smoke kind - a hangs _____ in _____ the

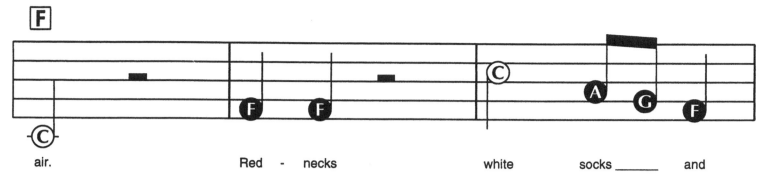

air.   Red - necks   white   socks _____ and

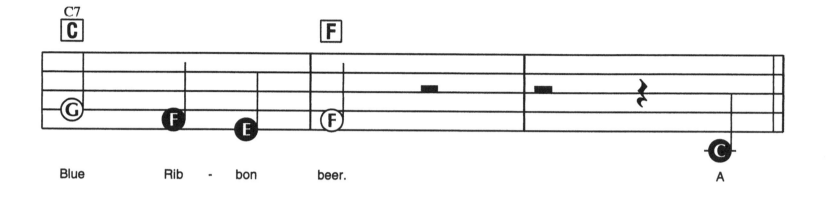

Blue   Rib - bon   beer.   A

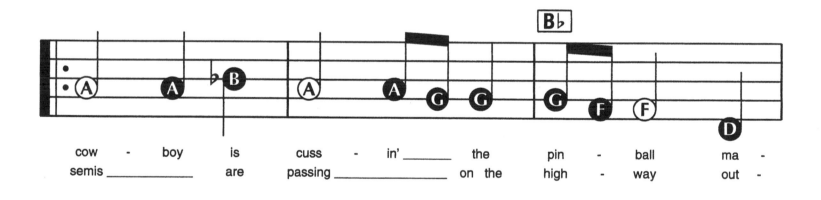

cow - boy   is   cuss - in' _____ the   pin - ball   ma -
semis _____ are   passing _____ on the   high - way   out -

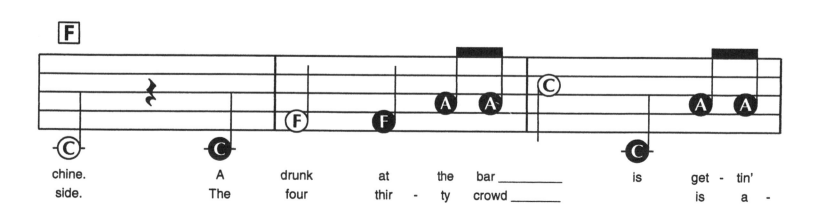

chine.   A   drunk   at   the   bar _____ is   get - tin'
side.   The   four   thir - ty   crowd _____ is   a -

noi - y   and _____   mean.   And,   some
bout   to _____   ar - rive.   The

guy   on   the phone _____   says   "I'll _____   be ____ home   soon _____
sun's   go - in' down _____   and   we'll   soon _____   all   be

dear."   Red - necks,   white   socks _____   and
here.   Red - necks,   white   socks _____   and

Blue   Rib - bon   beer.   No
Blue   Rib - bon   beer.

we   don't   fit   in _____   with   that   white   col - lar   crowd. _

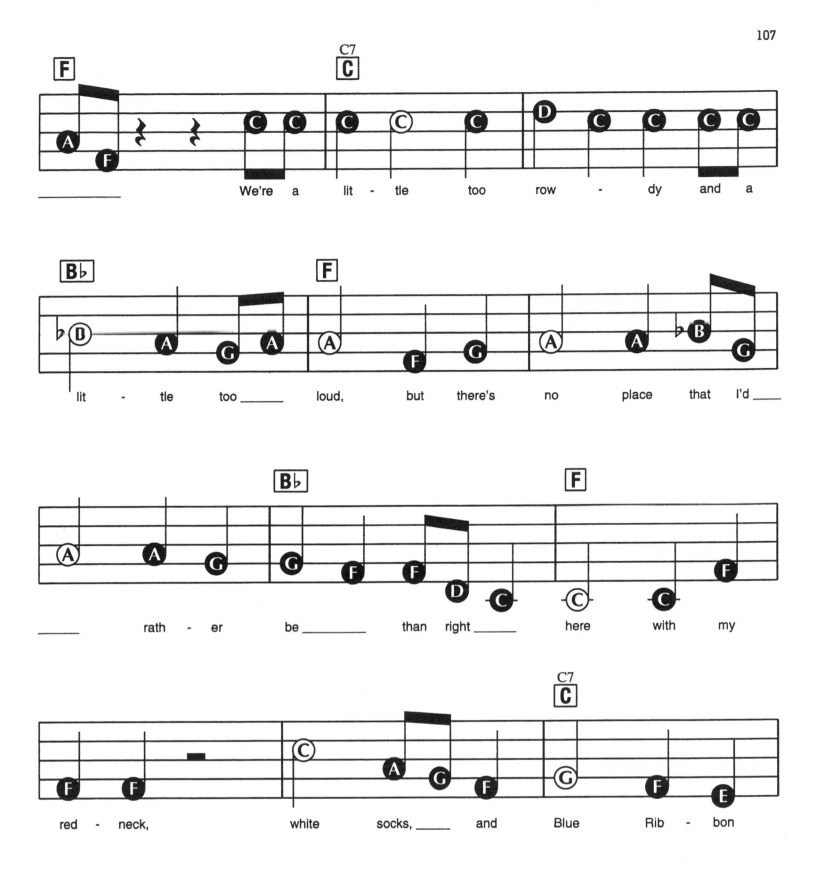

We're a lit - tle too row - dy and a lit - tle too _____ loud, but there's no place that I'd _____ _____ rath - er be _____ than right _____ here with my

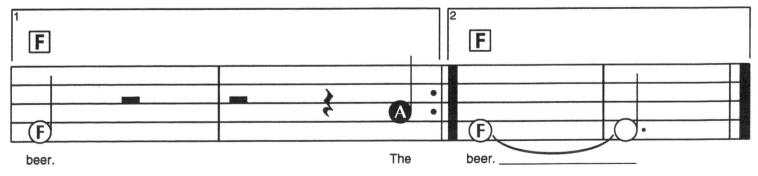

red - neck, white socks, _____ and Blue Rib - bon

beer. The beer. _____

Release Me

Registration 1
Rhythm: Country

Words and Music by Robert Yount,
Eddie Miller and Dub Williams

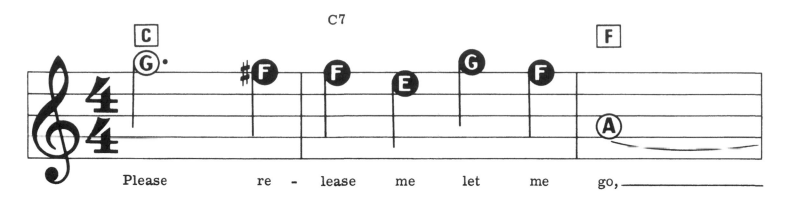

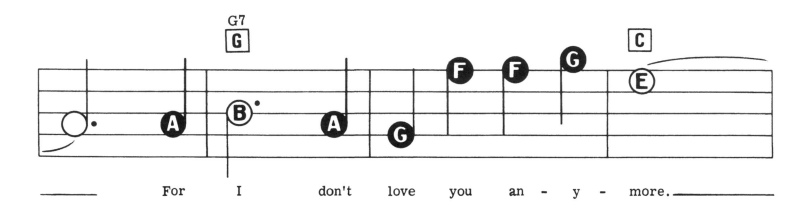

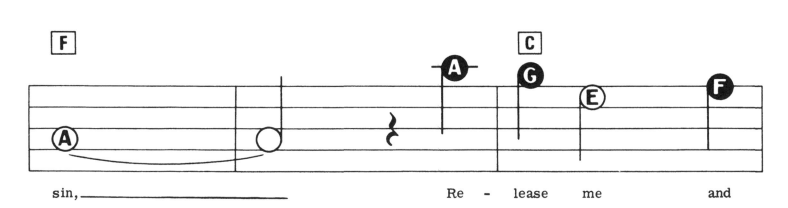

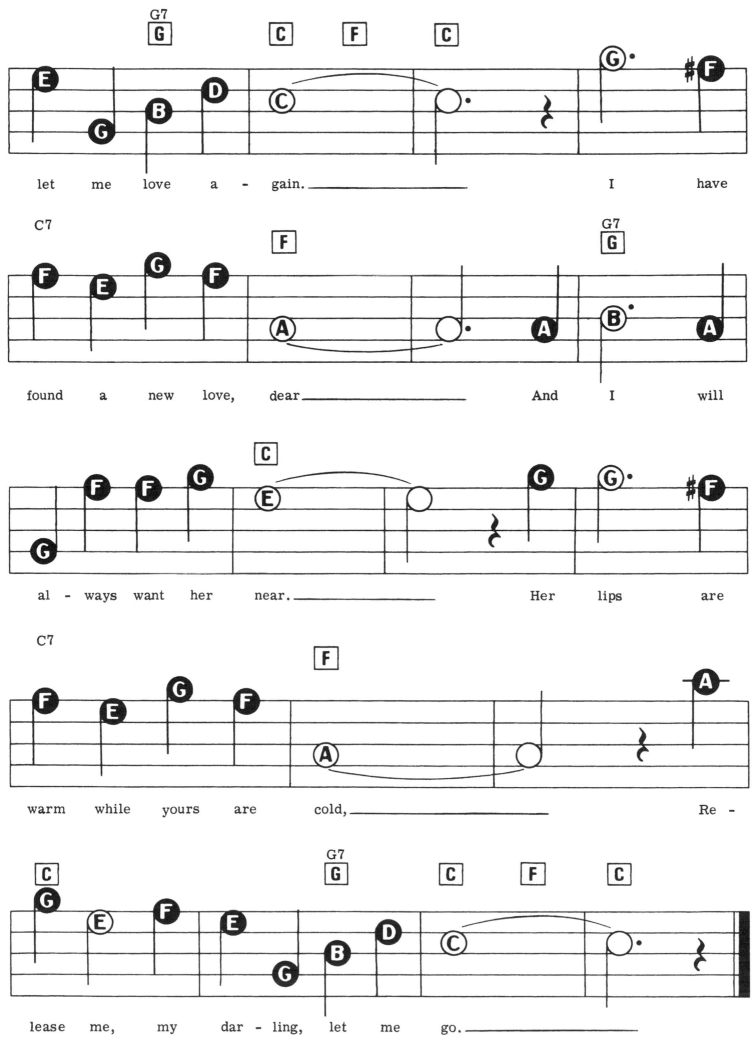

Ring of Fire

Registration 3
Rhythm: Rock

Words and Music by Merle Kilgore
and June Carter

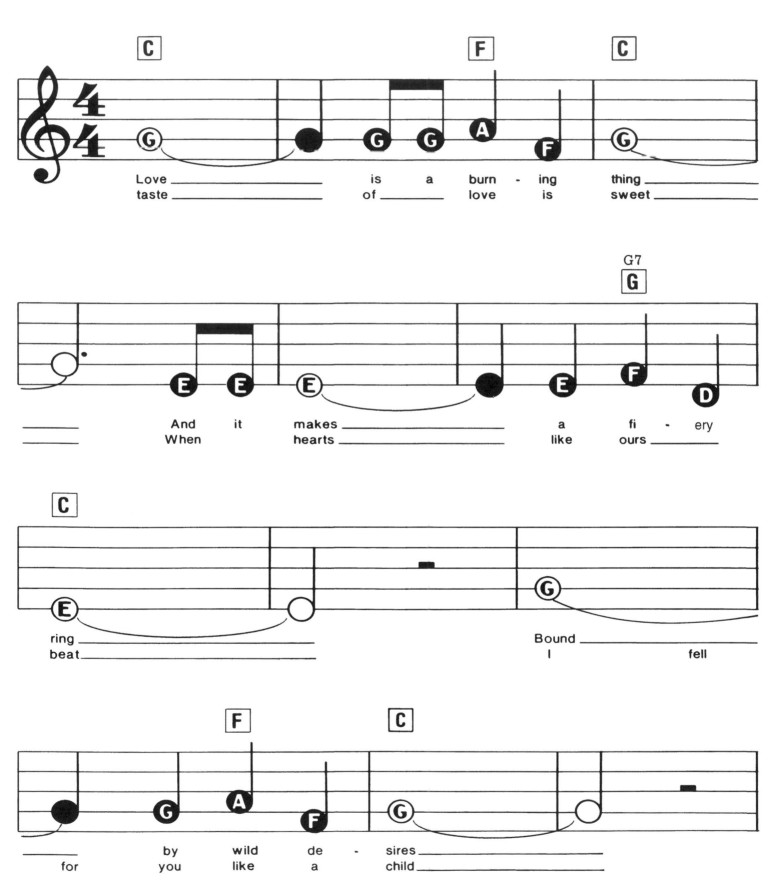

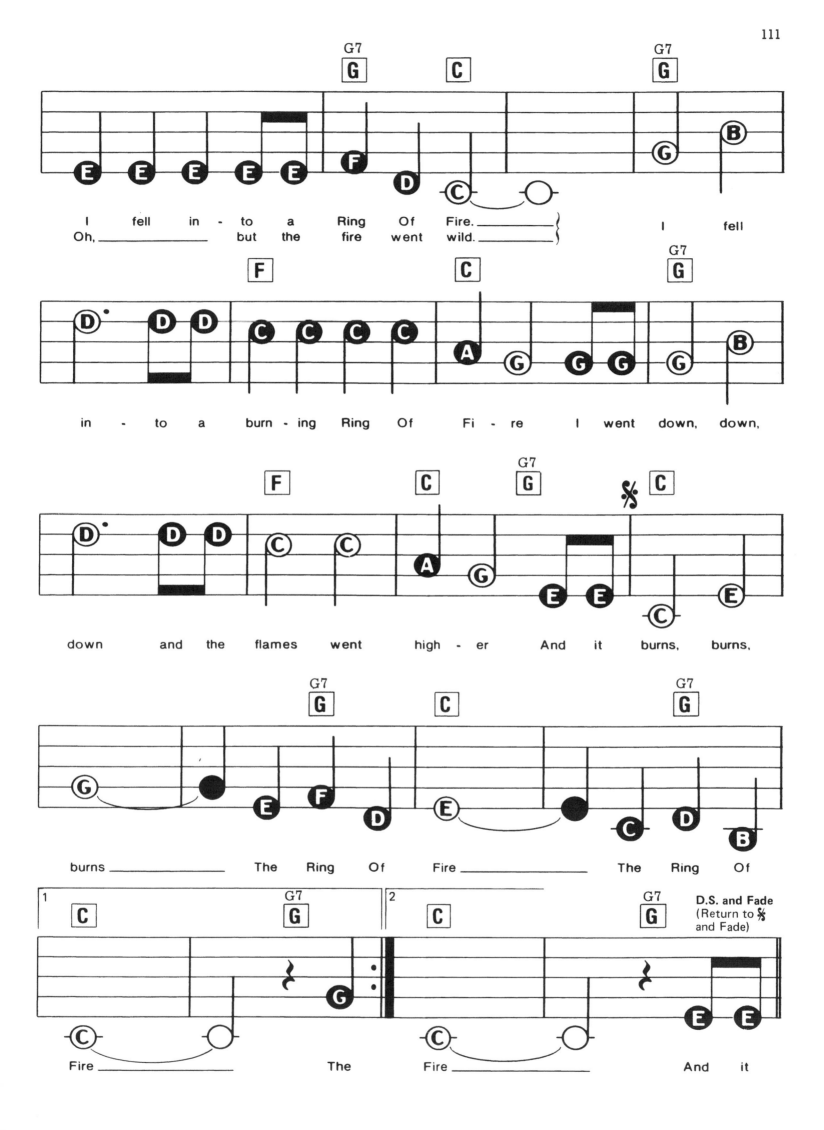

Room Full of Roses

Registration 5
Rhythm: Fox Trot or Country

Words and Music by
Tim Spencer

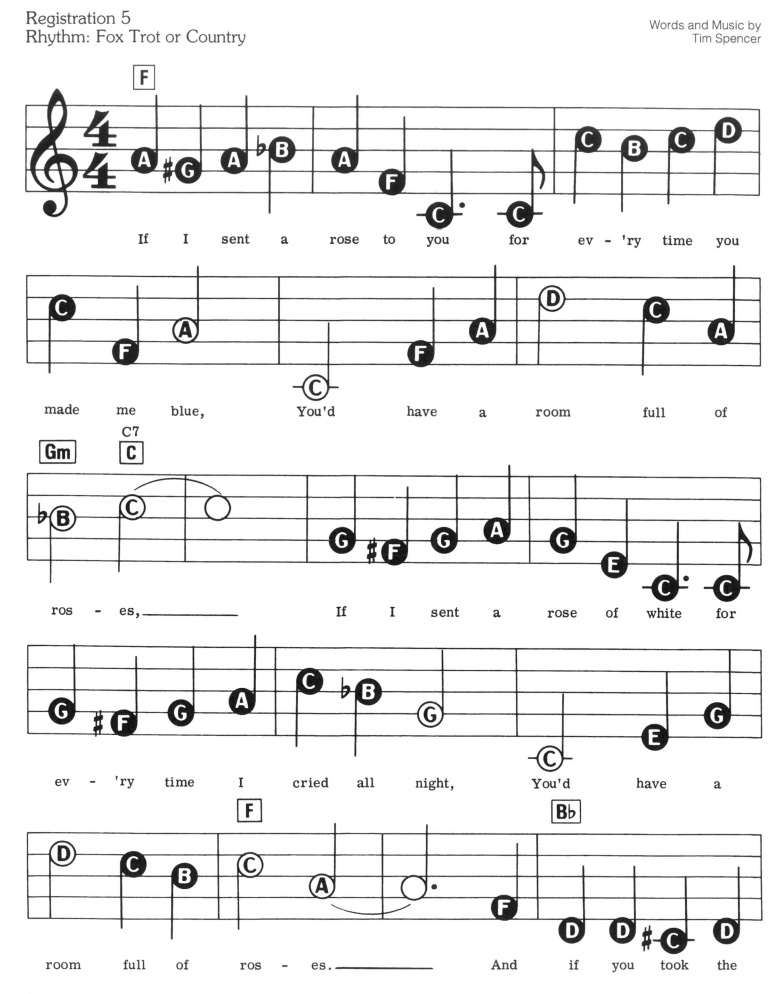

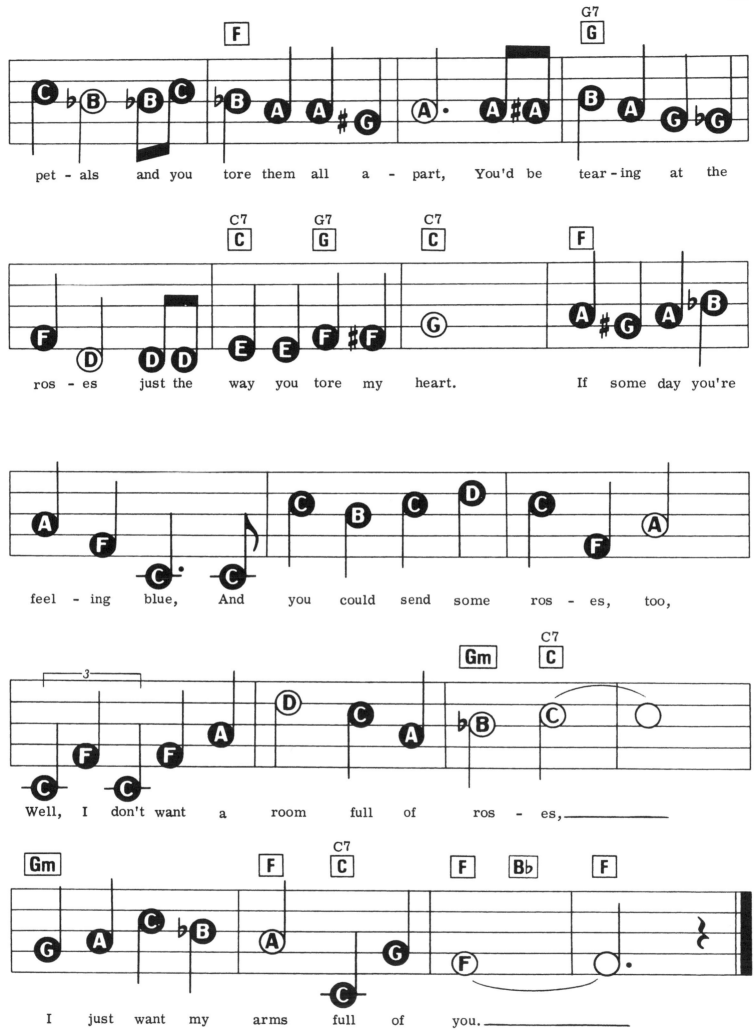

Southern Nights

Registration 4
Rhythm: Rock or Slow Rock

Words and Music by
Allen Toussaint

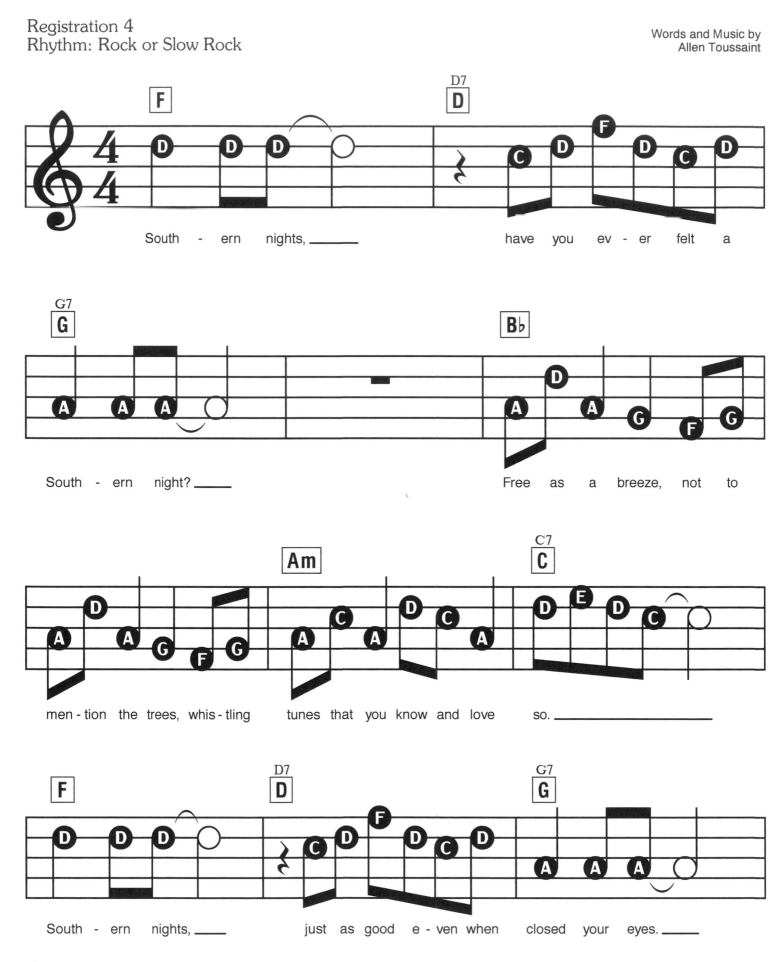

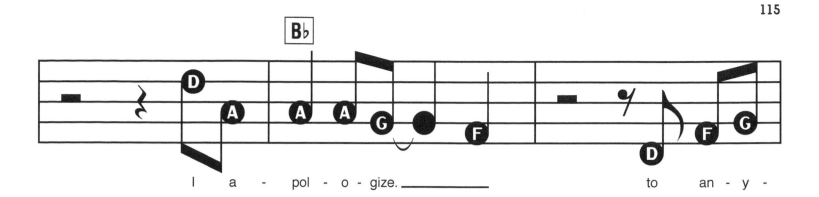

I a - pol - o - gize. _____ to an - y -

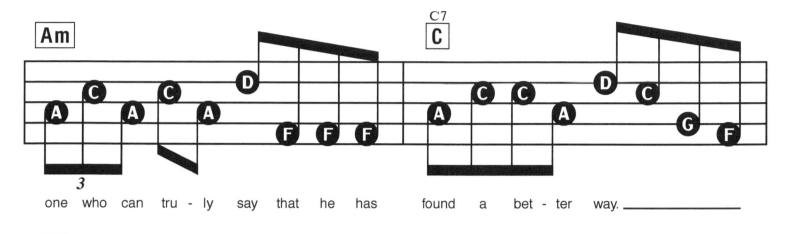

one who can tru - ly say that he has found a bet - ter way. _____

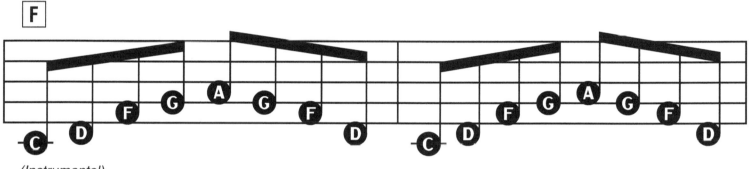

(Instrumental)

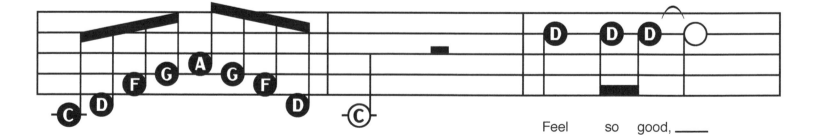

Feel so good, ___

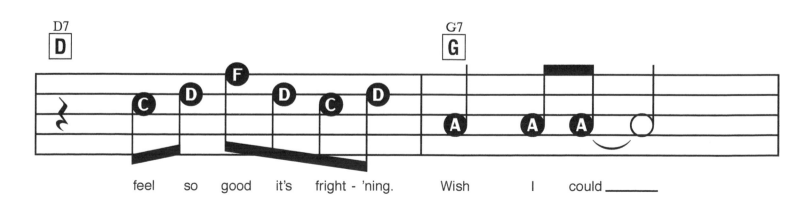

feel so good it's fright - 'ning. Wish I could _____

115

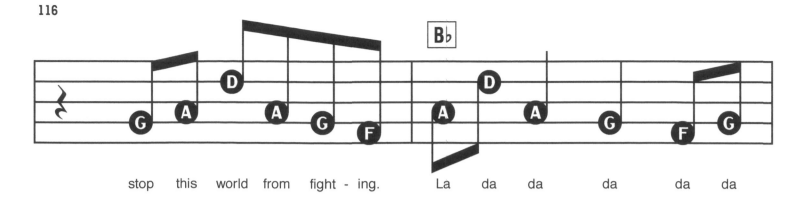

stop this world from fight - ing. La da da da da da

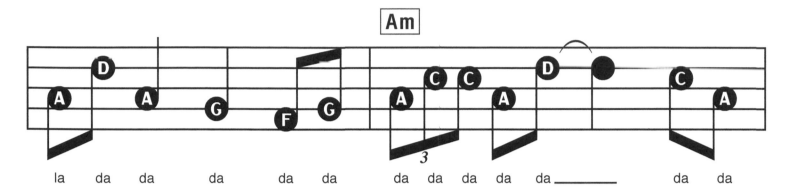

la da da da da da da da da da da _____ da da

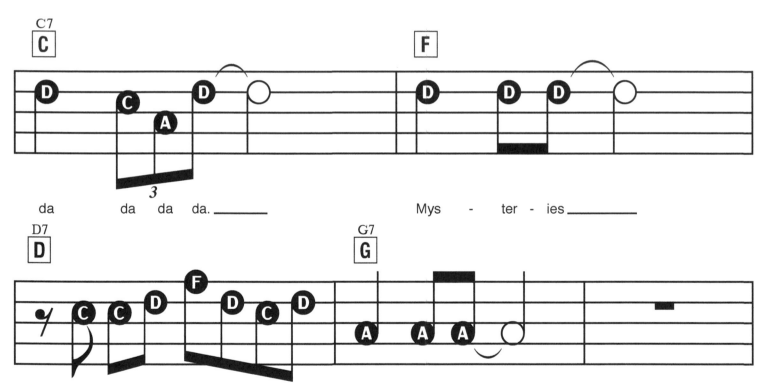

da da da da. _____ Mys - ter - ies _____

like this and man - y oth - ers in the trees _____

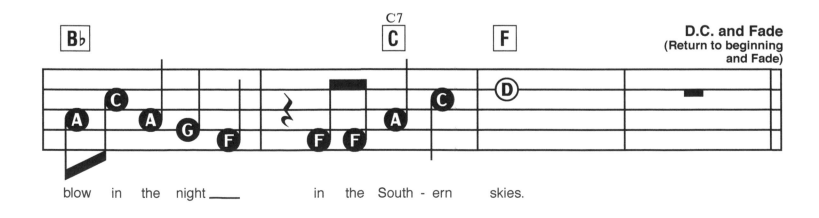

D.C. and Fade
(Return to beginning
and Fade)

blow in the night ___ in the South - ern skies.

Take This Job and Shove It

Registration 4
Rhythm: Country or Swing

Words and Music by
David Allen Coe

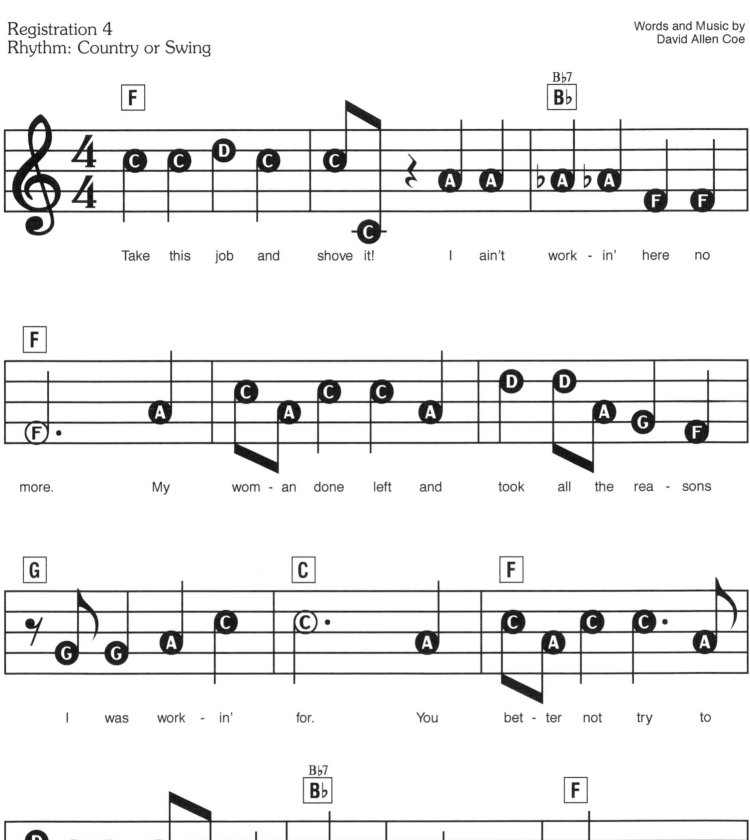

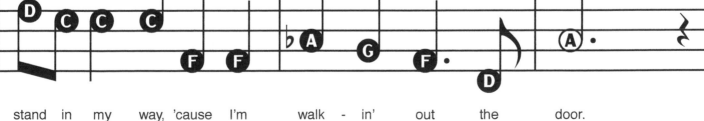

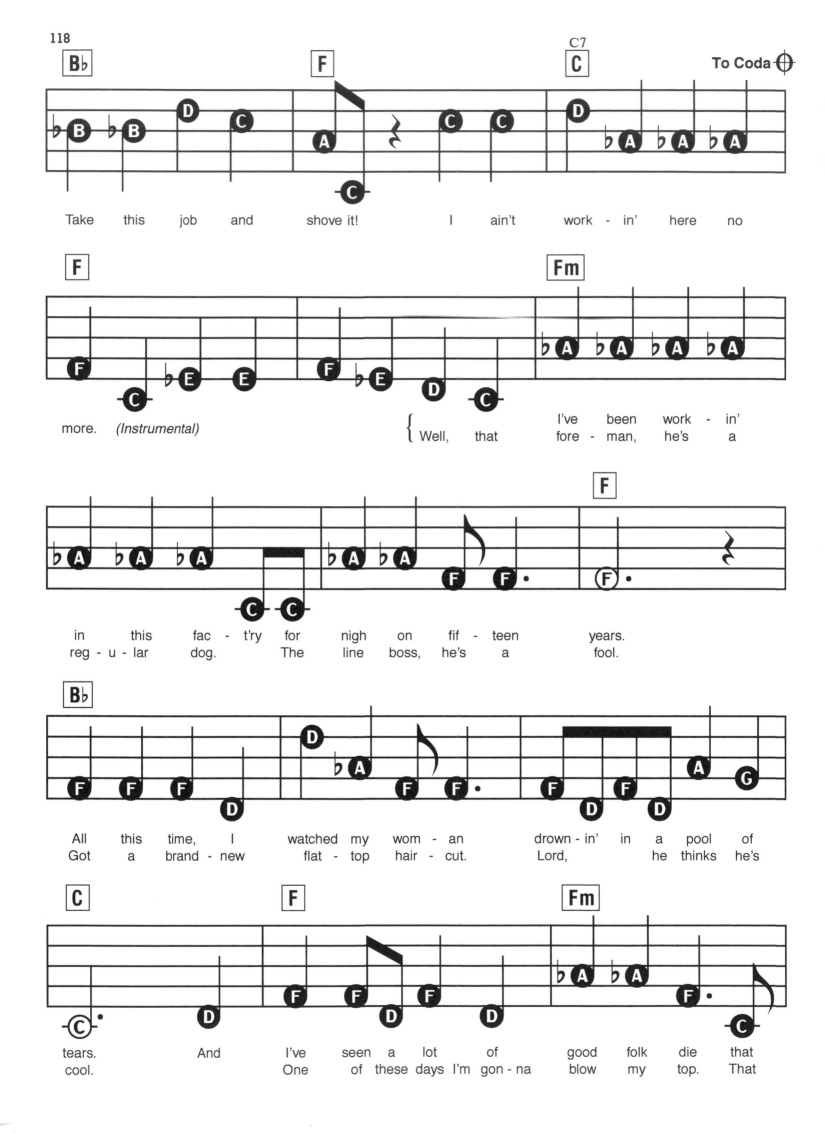

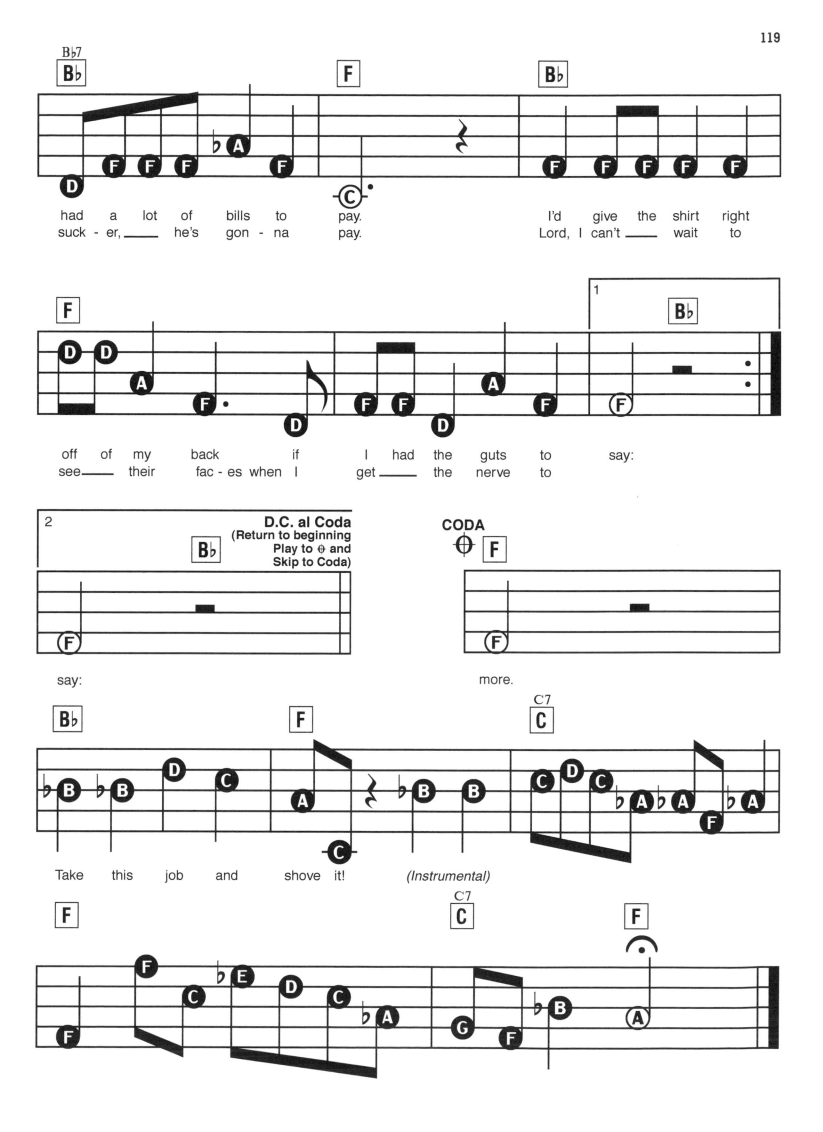

had a lot of bills to pay.
suck - er,___ he's gon - na pay.

I'd give the shirt right
Lord, I can't ___ wait to

off of my back if I had the guts to say:
see___ their fac - es when I get ___ the nerve to

D.C. al Coda
(Return to beginning
Play to ⊕ and
Skip to Coda)

say:

CODA

more.

Take this job and shove it! *(Instrumental)*

There's a Tear in My Beer

Registration 4
Rhythm: Fox Trot or Ballad

Words and Music by
Hank Williams

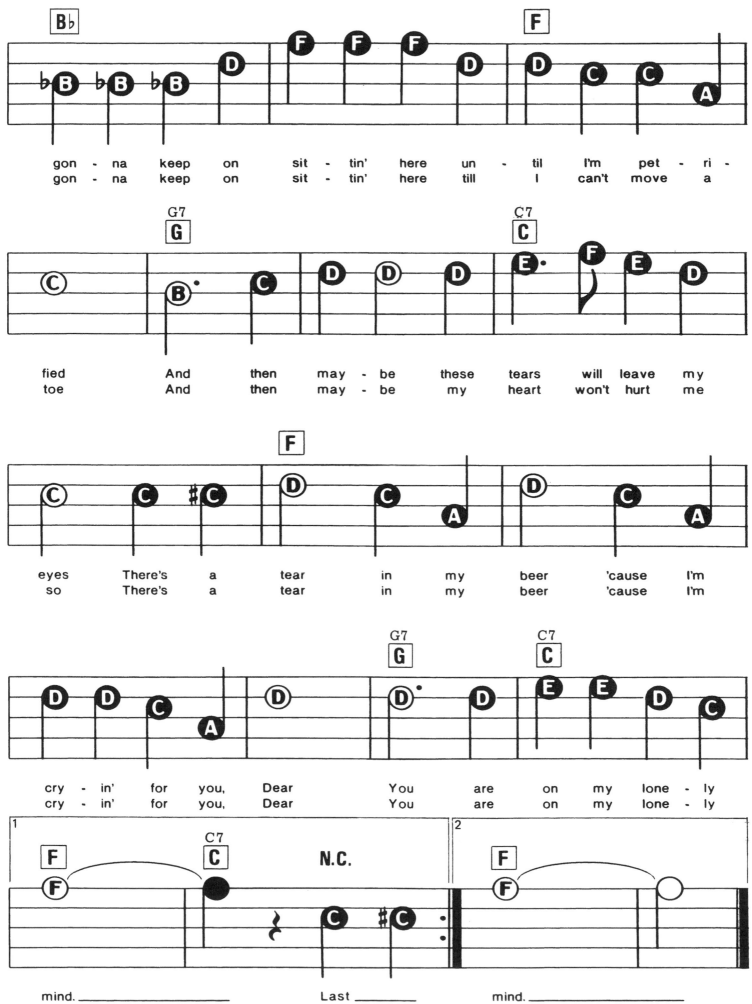

Whiskey River

Registration 2
Rhythm: Country Pop or Fox Trot

Words and Music by
J.B. Shinn III

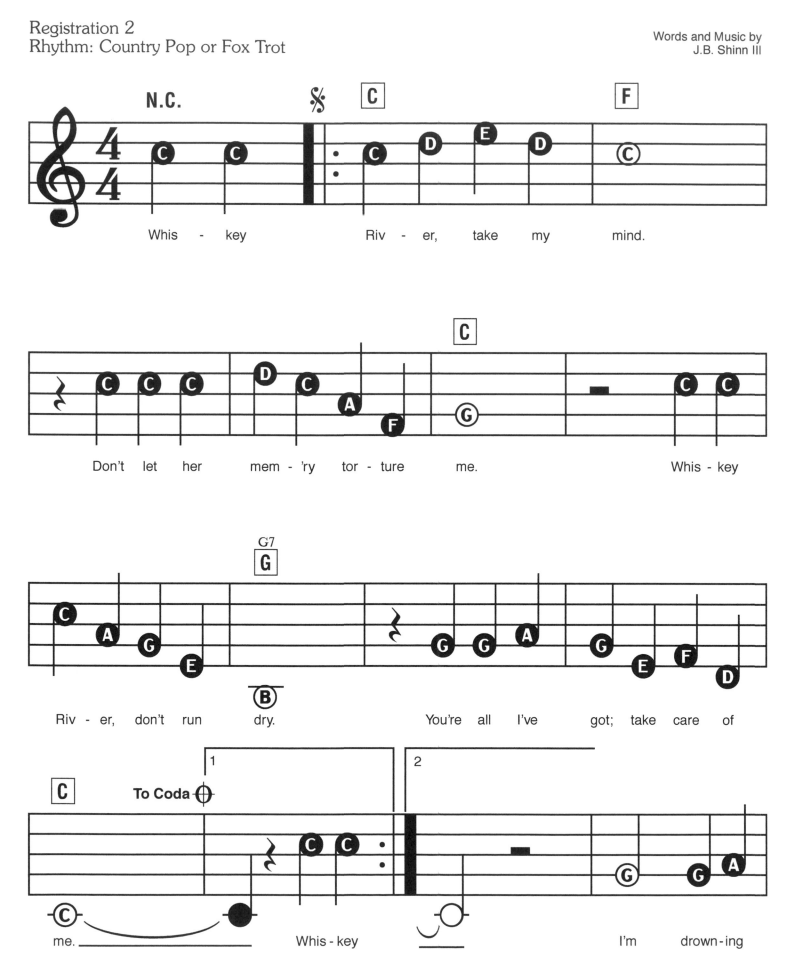

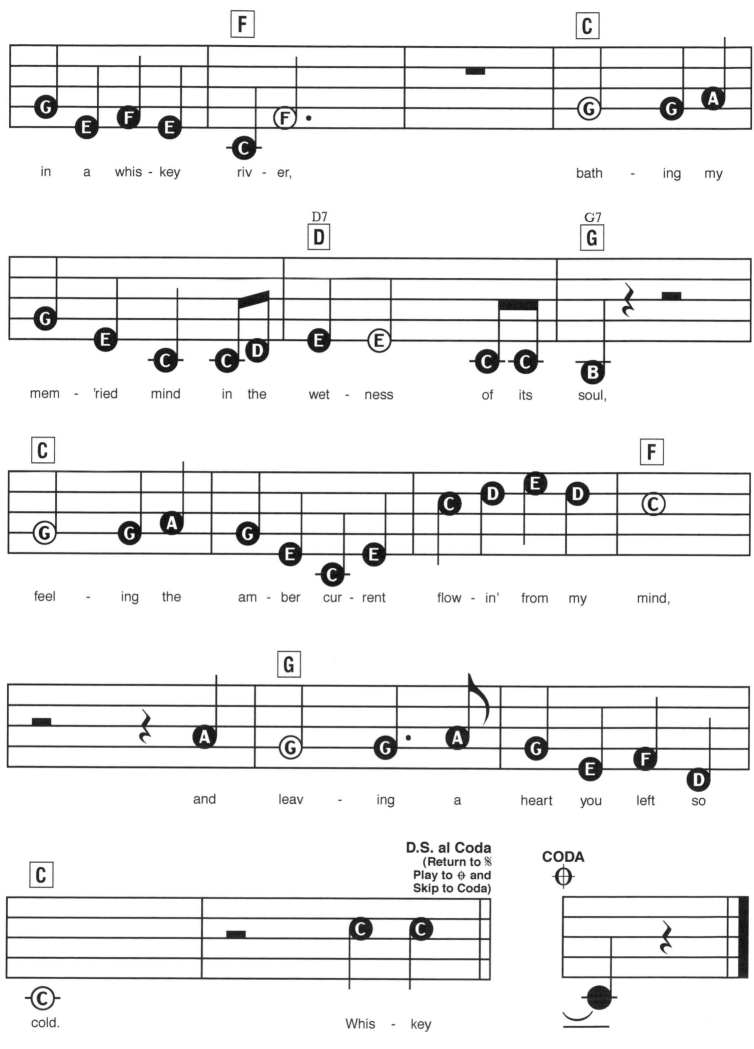

Witchita Lineman

Registration 9
Rhythm: 8-Beat, Pops, or Rock

Words and Music by
Jimmy Webb

N.C.

B♭

I am the line - man for the coun - ty,

Dm

Gm

and I drive the main road

Dm **Am** **G**

search - in' in the sun for an - oth - er o - ver -

D **Am**

load. I hear you sing - in' in the wires, _____

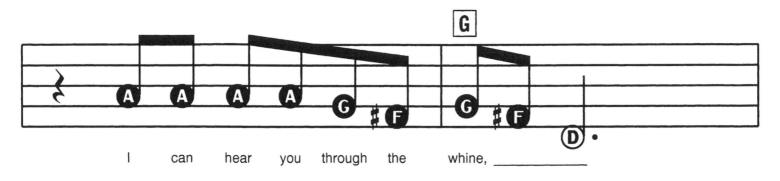

I can hear you through the whine, _____

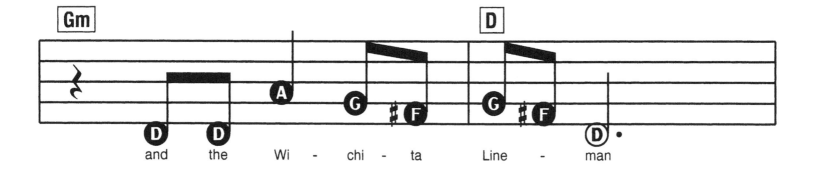

and the Wi - chi - ta Line - man

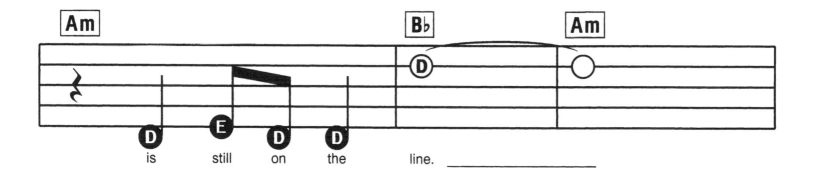

is still on the line. _____

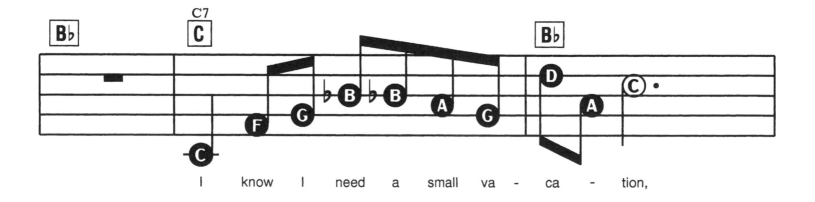

I know I need a small va - ca - tion,

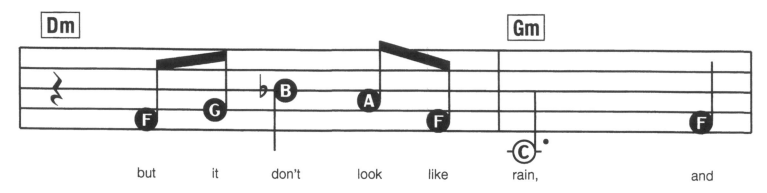

but it don't look like rain, and

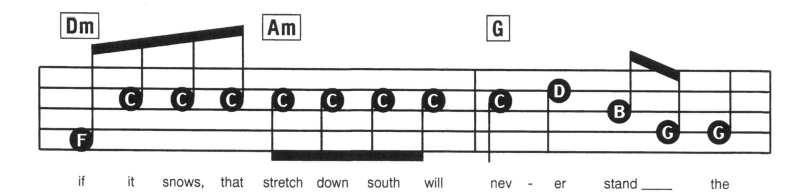

if it snows, that stretch down south will nev - er stand ____ the

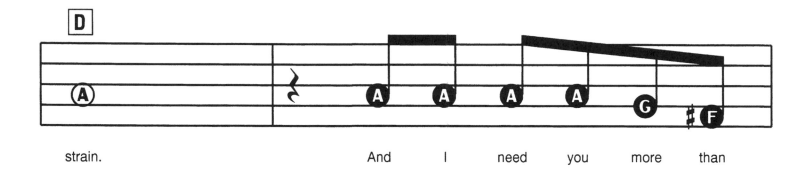

strain. And I need you more than

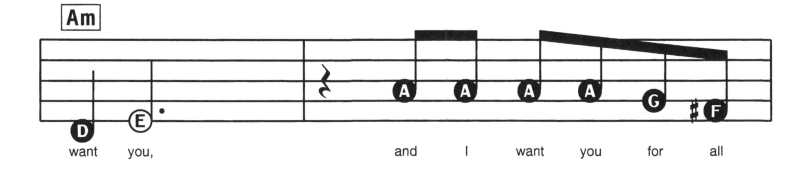

want you, and I want you for all

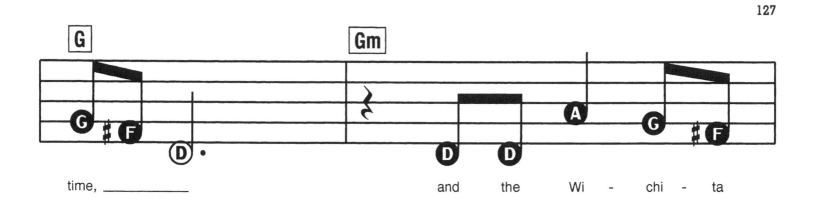

time, _____ and the Wi - chi - ta

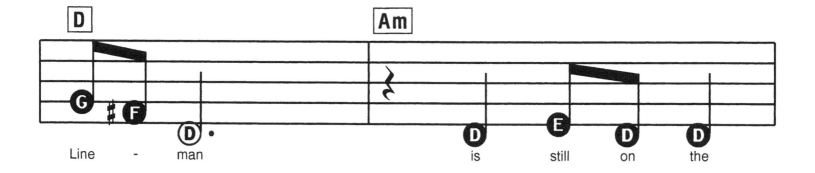

Line - man is still on the

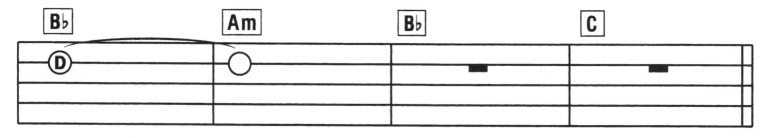

line._____

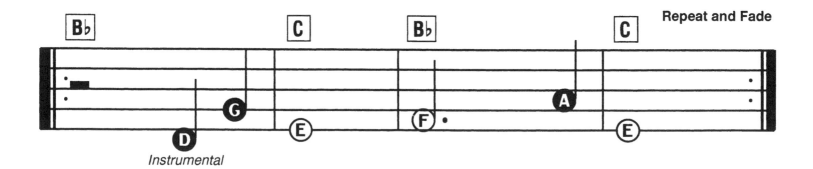

Instrumental

Repeat and Fade

FOR ORGANS, PIANOS & ELECTRONIC KEYBOARDS

E-Z PLAY® TODAY

E-Z PLAY® TODAY PUBLICATIONS

The E-Z Play® Today songbook series is the shortest distance between beginning music and playing fun!
Check out this list of highlights and visit balleonard.com for a complete listing of all volumes and songlists.

HAL•LEONARD®

Prices, contents and availability subject to change without notice

0421

330